TRACY EDWARDS

from

MILK

to

MEAT

Growing in Spiritual Maturity.
Building on a firm foundation

From Milk to Meat
Growing in Spiritual Maturity.
Building on a firm foundation

©Tracy Edwards

print ISBN: 978-1-09837-047-3
ebook ISBN: 978-1-09837-048-0

Tracy Edwards
P.O. BOX 110183
Aurora, CO 80042-0183
tannette623@gmail.com

Hebrews 5:11-14 NLT

There is much more we would like to say about this, but it is difficult to explain, especially since you are spiritually dull and don't seem to listen. You have been believers so long now that you ought to be teaching others. Instead, you need someone to teach you again the basic things about God's word. You are like babies who need milk and cannot eat solid food. For someone who lives on milk is still an infant and doesn't know how to do what is right. Solid food is for those who are mature, who through training have the skill to recognize the difference between right and wrong.

CONTENTS

FOREWORD   1

PROLOGUE   3

GRACE   5

FAITH   11

WHO AM I?   17

RELATIONSHIP AND INTIMACY   27

PRAYER AND FASTING   35

THE ANATOMY OF A SERVANT   47

WHO CAN RIVAL GOD?   57

REFERENCES   69

FOREWORD

Apostle Tracy Edwards is truly a devoted Woman of God, a great sister and friend to me, my wife and family. Apostle Tracy has always shown integrity, humility and honesty and she is not afraid to help others to reach their goals. Tracy is called to be a leader mandated for this time and season in her teaching and as an author through the anointing of the Holy Spirit. I give praise and honor to our God for allowing Apostle Tracy to birth this fresh and authentic book. From Milk to Meat, Growing in Spiritual Maturity, Building on a Firm Foundation, Apostle Tracy shared insight and revelation directly from our Heavenly Father on Grace, Faith, Who am I, Relationship and Intimacy, Fasting and Prayer, The Anatomy of a servant and Who can rival God. This book is for everyone, (newly saved and for those who have been walking with the Lord for a while) to read and re-read this book frequently, individually or in small groups and discuss how we can grow and mature in our relationship with God. Thank you, my sister, for your obedience and hearing the voice of the Lord to write From Milk to Meat for our spiritual growth and knowing we can build on a firm foundation. My prayer is that this book and the others to follow to accomplish and reach the masses in and for the Kingdom of God.

Bishop Stephen Baker
Power House Christian Fellowship
Aurora, Colorado

I have known Tracy over 20 years. Besides her sweet spirit, she is a very intelligent and versatile woman of God. She brings a sense of peace and acceptance to any room she enters. It is of no surprise that she has written this book and even more to follow. Her passion for God and His people is apparent the moment you meet her. Her faith in God has surely produced a book that will acquaint readers with terms that we here regularly and frequently in our local churches. It is so refreshing to read material that is identifiable. Her ability to rightly divide the word of truth is evident and it credits her work as an author. She addresses the total man in a way that challenges you to dig deeper, sacrifice more and fight harder to live a life beyond the soul of man. Grace, Faith, Who am I and Who can rival God are but a few chapters in this book that will clarify any fallacy you've been introduced to. A must read for every library. Hosea 4:10(a) "My people are destroyed for lack of knowledge". Thank you, Tracy, for your obedience and discipline to give the world gospel truths that continue to challenge me daily.

Pastor Sonya Baker
Power House Christian Fellowship
Aurora, Colorado

PROLOGUE

Many of us have left the gates running without the proper training and conditioning. We may be able to run the race but are we running well? Is our running effective? Do we feel equipped on this journey? All the Glory to God for giving us everything we need. "By His divine power, God has given us everything we need for living a godly life. We have received all of this by coming to know him, the one who called us to himself by means of his marvelous glory and excellence." 2 Peter 1:3 NLT

GRACE

"For by works of the law no human being will be justified in his sight, since through the law comes knowledge of sin. But now the righteousness of God has been manifested apart from the law, although the Law and the Prophets bear witness to it — the righteousness of God through faith in Jesus Christ for all who believe. For there is no distinction: for all have sinned and fall short of the glory of God, and are justified by his grace as a gift, through the redemption that is in Christ Jesus . . . . "

Romans 3:20-24 ESV

According to the Word of God, grace is the divine influence upon the heart and its reflection in our lives. The Old Testament word for grace is Khane (Strong's 2580) meaning graciousness (kindness, favor), pleasant, precious. In the New Testament the word used is Kharece (khar'-ece/Strong's 5485) meaning benefit, favor, gift, gracious, joy or pleasure.

Grace is commonly defined as unmerited favor or a free unconditional granting of God's blessings. God gives us grace to save us, set us free from the bondage of sin, and make us whole. Grace gives us provision, protection, peace, joy, health, and wealth. God gives us the best definition of grace in John 3:16 KJV "For God so loved the world, that he gave his only begotten Son, that whosoever believeth in him should not perish, but have everlasting life." Grace loves.... freely gives....and is unselfish. I'm reminded of a mnemonic used to explain grace as Gods Riches At Christ Expense! This is very fitting to describe how Jesus gave Himself so that we can be called the children of God. Under the old covenant, we were governed by the "law" but now we are "under" the law of grace. Gods' grace not only has the power to save us but is also the same power that keeps us in His will and supplies us with the strength to do the work of God (I Corinthians 15:10).

Understanding the gift of grace that God has given us changes our perspective on life itself. God, we pray that you will show us how your grace has changed us and we pray that you will empower us to do the things you have purposed us to do. Let's look at some biblical examples of grace in action:

This first example of grace is found in the story of Jonah. Jonah is identified as the son of the prophet Amittai (2Kings 14:25/Jonah 1:1). Jonah is best known for the book bearing his name. We read in this book how Jonah attempted to run away from Gods call that instructed him to announce Gods judgment against the people of Nineveh. Jonah made a conscious decision to go in the opposite direction because he was not fond of the people of Nineveh. He knew that God would be gracious and merciful, slow to anger and of great kindness (Jonah 4:2). Jonah deemed the Ninevites unworthy of God's grace or mercy. In Chapter 2 it tells us how Jonah "cried out" in prayer to God after being swallowed by a great fish. Jonah himself prayed for Gods mercy and experienced His grace. Though Jonah was obedient in delivering the Word of God to the people of Nineveh, he did so not wanting God to show them the same mercy and grace he recently received. There are times when it will seem easier to love and have faith in a God whom we've never seen face to face then it is to love those created in His image. Some of us display His beauty different from others. Sometimes it takes a little effort to see God's beauty in people and other times it seems almost impossible. We must remain consistent in obeying one of the greatest commandments Jesus gave us and that is to love. Jonah did not exhibit the fruit of the Spirit as described in Galatians 5:22-23. Instead, he showed the fruit of his sinful nature, the fruit of his flesh. Because of his anger and hatred towards the people of Nineveh he missed out on one of the most extraordinary revivals ever seen. When we grudgingly give or refuse to extend God's grace to others, it sets up in us a root of bitterness and anger in us. We are then not able to fully experience the peace that God wants us to have. The peace Jesus came here to give us (John 14:27). It may be easy for us to point a harsh finger at others when they fall short, but we must be careful not to fall into the same temptation ourselves (Galatians 6:1). Paul in Galatians 6:1 lets us know that when our brother or sister stray off of the right path we must restore them back gently and humbly. We should love our neighbors as ourselves (Gal. 5:14).

(Prayerfully ask God to show you areas in your life where you have failed to show grace to others) Father, I pray that you teach me how to love others like you love me at all times. Let me be quick to listen and slow to speak. God, I ask you to give me the strength to forgive others that may not act according to Your way. I know that You have forgiven me, and I pray that I will be quick to forgive others.

Another example of grace is King David, who spent many years of his life running from King Saul. After the death of King Saul and his son Jonathan (David's very best friend) at the hands of the Philistines, David sought out for someone in Saul's family he could bless. David says in 2 Samuel 9:1 "Is there yet any who is left of the house of Saul, that I may show him kindness [Kheh'-sed-favour, goodness, kindness, merciful](Strong's 2617) for Jonathan's sake?" Johnathan's son, Mephibosheth (2 Samuel 4:4), who was crippled after the nurse caring for him dropped him when she heard the news of his father's and grandfather's death, was still alive and lived in Lo Debar. Thus, Mephibosheth the lame son of Jonathan was brought to David from Lo Debar. Lo-Debar meaning pasture-less and considered a very low place-a "nothing town". David invited Mephibosheth to sit at his table to eat and to wear the finest clothing. Maybe you can identify with what Mephibosheth is feeling here. You may not have been crippled physically but maybe someone has hurt you mentally or even spiritually. Can you imagine coming from such a low place in your life? A place of little or no hope for better days? But now you are invited to the Kings table. Psalms 23 says that God has prepared a table for us. He is ready to fill our cups, all of the empty spaces in which life has depleted us. You may not feel as though you are worthy to come to the table. Even Mephibosheth didn't count himself as worthy. When he came to David he fell on his face and laid himself down in deep respect referring to himself as David's servant. (See 2 Samuel 9:5-7) It is God's grace that invites us to the table not because we hold a title or position. It is not because we are so good or have accomplished great things. It is not by our works but it is by the finished work of Jesus. Jesus is our righteousness and He has made us worthy. 2 Corinthians 9:8 NLT says that God will generously provide all we need. Then you will always have everything you need, and plenty left over to share with others. Grace is like an elixir of life. When we pour out our grace on others it in turn gives us an abundant life full of peace, joy, love and happiness. Grace then is not only the blessed gift of eternal life but it is a gift from God that contains everything we need that pertains to life. There are so many times I've said, "I may not have everything I want but God gives me everything I need". . God had to elevate my thoughts and my speech. He let me know that the things I want pale in comparison to the blessings He wants to give me. In essence, the needs that God supplies for me are far greater in value when compared to the small minded things I want. Just like David snatched Mephibosheth out of Lo Debar to sit in high places, God seeks to do the same for us. I'm sure David did not take the time to ask if this was what he wanted. He recognized what he needed. David poured out Kheh'-sed without measure. He gave Mephibosheth his very best. We receive the grace of God without measure and we should be eager to share this gift freely with others. Is the grace that God wonderfully extends to us the same grace that we extend to others? In the story of the prodigal son (Luke 15:11-32) Jesus gives us an example of the good Father so full of grace who freely extends it to his son while the older brother refuses to extend any grace towards his brother. Galatians 6:4 NLT says that we should "pay careful attention to [our] own work, for then [we] will get the satisfaction of a job well done, and [we] won't need to compare [ourselves] to anyone else."

Again, prayerfully ask God how you can show grace to others you encounter everyday: God I ask that you show me opportunities to display Your kindness to others. Thank you for lifting me from a low place. I need Your help Father to encourage my brothers and sisters that they also may be lifted by Your Love.

A third example of grace is Paul (Saul), a Pharisee who studied under Gamaliel (Acts 22:3-13) and knew and observed the law like no other. He was very zealous to honor God in everything even to the point of persecuting those who followed after Jesus' teachings. God interrupted Paul on the Damascus Road to shower him with His grace. After Pauls' eyes were opened God commanded Paul to get up, go be baptized and have his sins washed away by calling on the name of the Lord! There are many times we may feel we are on a good path yet we are blindly walking through life. It is the grace of God that opens up our blinded eyes, stops us from going on this path of destruction and places us on the right path. Paul experienced God's grace like no other on the road to Damascus. We can have the same life changing experience when we acknowledge Jesus as our Savior. In 1 Timothy 1:12-14 Paul confessed that a lot of the things he was doing against the followers of Jesus was done in ignorance. Paul acknowledged that it was the mercy of God that now filled him with faith and love and it was all because of Jesus. In the letter to the Galatians (Chapter 4) Paul gives a wonderful picture of law and grace. He contrasts Abraham's children, Ishmael, the son born to Hagar, Sarah's slave, and Isaac, the son born to Sarah. Ishmael, represents the law which was conceived by human hands in an attempt to fulfill God's promise. On the other hand, the promised child, Isaac represents grace for he was conceived by the work and will of God. Galatians 4:30 says to get rid of the slave and her child for they shall not share the inheritance with the son of the free woman. We are saved and set free by the sacrificial work of Jesus not by our human efforts. We are rescued from the penalty of death by God's grace when we believe. We cannot take credit for anything. (Ephesians 2:8) God's grace is enough! When we try (in our efforts) to find favor with God by obeying the law we will be cut off from God. You have fallen from God's grace. Grace is replacing our human weakness with the Strength of God. God sent Paul forth to preach His word to the Gentiles. Paul understood it was the strength of God that allowed him to do this great work. Three times Paul prayed for God to remove the "thorn" in his life and God's response was that His grace is sufficient. We all have something in our lives that we feel is our "Achilles heel". I'm not sure what the thorn was in Paul's life but I do know it was detrimental enough for him to pray that God would take it away. There are many things in my life that I would love for my Daddy to just speak and poof they are gone but I can hear His sweet voice say to me "My grace is enough". 1 Corinthians 15:10 shows us it is God's grace working in us to accomplish His great works. It is through the grace of God that we are able to complete the work God has sent us here to do. For we are all given a measure of grace (Ephesians 4:7). We will not do this in our own strength but by the grace and power of God. Grace is receiving the strength of God in the place of our weakness. We are able to do all things through Christ who gives us the strength. Don't worry about tomorrow because God has given us the grace we need in this hour. He says that His mercies are new every morning. God will give us our daily bread.

(Prayerfully ask God to keep you in your walk of life): God I acknowledge that there are times when I do not ask you what direction I should go. Thank you for forgiving me. Please help me Holy Spirit to acknowledge God in all of my ways and to follow after You. I ask You to show me how to receive your grace to endure life's challenges. I know that it is because of Your grace that I am able to accomplish all of the things You purposed for me to do.

With our newfound realization of the gift of grace given to us, we should not use this gift to satisfy our sinful nature but use our freedom to serve one another in love (Romans 6). Grace is not something we've earned based on our good works. Grace is a gift that God has given us freely. Not taking into account things we have done or will do. God counted Abraham righteous not because he "earned" it but because he believed God (Genesis 15:6). Abraham believed God was faithful to keep His promises...faithful to rescue him from all troubles...faithful to provide for him...faithful to protect him from dangers seen and unseen and He still is faithful. God has not and will not change. He is the same yesterday, today and forever more. Will you believe God today? Receive His grace.

FAITH

"Now faith is the substance of things hoped for, the evidence of things not seen."

Hebrews 11:1 KJV

Faith is defined as a complete trust or confidence in someone or something. Another definition of faith is a strong belief in God or in the doctrine of a religion based on spiritual apprehension rather than proof. Merriam-Webster Dictionary defines faith as a belief and trust in and loyalty to God, a belief in the traditional doctrines of a religion, or a firm belief in something for which there is no proof. In the book of Hebrews, Chapter 11, God gives us a wonderful insight into faith by telling us that faith is the substance of things hoped for, the evidence of things not seen (KJV). The faith given to us by our gracious Father is the foundation which His Grace and Mercy have paved the way for. It is because of our faith (belief) in God (Jesus) that we have a firm foundation. The word foundation is defined as the load bearing part of a building. Psalms 62:1-2 says, "I wait quietly before God, for my victory comes from him. He alone is my rock and my salvation, my fortress where I will never be shaken"(NLT). Jesus is our unshakable foundation. When we have faith in God we should trust him without hesitation knowing that He is not only the One bearing the load but the One doing all of the work. Can you imagine that type of faith? Faith where no matter what storms are blowing or quakes are rumbling attempting to shake me to my core, I can still wait quietly on God knowing that the victory is already won. A faith that knows whatever work He has sent me to do, He will accomplish through me and give me the grace to see it to completion.

The opposite of faith is unbelief. Hebrews 3:19 recounts how the children of Israel were not able to enter the rest of God because of their unbelief and Mark 6:5-6 tells us that Jesus was only able to do a few miracles in his hometown because of the people's unbelief. Jesus was amazed at their unbelief. Is it possible that we can limit the manifestation of the Power of God through our unbelief? Could it be that we are hindering blessings because we refuse to have faith in the All-Powerful Mighty God who wants to give us His everything? We already know through the Word that it is impossible to please God without faith. To be without is to be void of something. But God has given us faith. In fact, He has given us all things that pertains to life. It is because of Israel's unbelief and their refusal to receive the gift of salvation they were cut off and the Gentiles were grafted in from a wild olive tree. However, when the children of Israel believe (have faith) in Jesus, accepting the offer of salvation, they will be grafted back in (Romans 11:23).

One might think my faith is not where it needs to be. We can cry out like the Father in Mark 9:22-24. The father cried out, "I do believe but help me overcome my unbelief." What is he saying here? I want to believe without any wavering but there is something in me that questions if You are willing to do this great thing for me? God, please help me! The conversation between this desperate father and a loving compassionate Jesus always makes me think of myself. I am desperate for help but I do not always trust that God is willing to help me. It is not that I do not believe He can do it but will He do it for me? The answer is unequivocally YES! God is not only able but He is willing. The word of God says that we must walk by faith and not by sight (2 Corinthians 5:7). We must keep our eyes on Jesus as He leads and guides us through this life. Life has many distractions and it is the enemy's goal to keep us from our righteous walk with God. The enemy does not want the Word of God planted in the "good ground" of our hearts. In Luke 8:12, the seeds that fell on the foot path the devil came and took them away from their hearts to prevent them from believing and being saved. The enemy does not even want us to hear the Word and what we do hear he constantly seeks to steal and choke out of us with the cares of this world. Satan knows that if we hear the Word of God and then believe the Word we can tear down and destroy every lie he's ever told. In Matthew 14:24-31 as the disciples were on the boat in the middle of the sea they saw Jesus walking on the water in the midst of a storm. The disciples' immediate response was fear thinking Jesus was a ghost. However, Jesus reassured them that He was not a ghost and He was there with them. In the midst of the storm, I love Peter's response. While they were being tossed by the wind and the waves, Peter's focus was on Jesus. As long as Peter kept his eyes on Jesus he could also perform the miraculous act of walking on water. Sadly, when Peter began to focus on the surrounding storm, instead of the One who has power over the storm, he began to sink. Jesus rescued Peter but asked why did Peter doubt? When we put our complete confidence (faith) in Jesus we can be reassured that there is no storm He can't calm, no situation He can't handle.

God has demonstrated over and over again how trustworthy He is. Psalms 78:13-22, 32 (NLT) recounts the miraculous provisions he provided for the children of Israel. "For he divided the sea and led them through, making the water stand up like walls! In the daytime he led them by a cloud, and all night by a pillar of fire. He split open the rocks in the wilderness to give them water, as from a gushing spring. He made streams pour from the rock, making the waters flow down like a river! Yet they kept on sinning against him, rebelling against the Most High in the desert. They stubbornly tested God in their hearts, demanding the foods they craved. They even spoke against God himself, saying, "God can't give us food in the wilderness. Yes, he can strike a rock so water gushes out, but he can't give his people bread and meat." When the Lord heard them, he was furious. The fire of his wrath burned against Jacob. Yes, his anger rose against Israel, for they did not believe God or trust him to care for them. But in spite of this, the people kept sinning. Despite his wonders, they refused to trust him." After all they had seen and experienced with God they still did not believe! If

God can split the sea and deliver them from the hands of the Egyptians why can He not supply all they needed while in the wilderness and beyond?

In our lives today, how many times have we experienced God move mightily in our lives? Supply our daily needs? Take care of our love ones? Why do we still doubt when we are in strange places? We still serve the Mighty God who is able to do all things but fail. He is willing! We just need to have faith the size of a mustard seed. The key word here is "have" which means to possess or take hold of. Jesus tells his disciples if they have faith as small as a mustard seed mountains will move. In Luke 17:5, the disciples cried out to the Lord to increase (add to) their faith. Where is your faith? We grow in faith by the different situations and trials we go through in life. Prayerfully ask God to increase your faith: Lord we ask in the mighty name of Jesus that you will give us the faith that pleases You. Let us trust without wavering regardless of the storms that may come.

It is because of our faith in Jesus that we are made right with God (Galatians 2:16). Be ready to live a life full of faith. Wherever we are in our faith walk, God desires to take us higher for His Glory. Faith is an action word. James 2:14 lets us know that faith without works (good deeds) is dead. The gift of faith God graciously gives us is alive and ready to work. God's desire is to move through us so that men can see and glorify Him. Help us Oh God to walk by faith and not by sight (2 Corinthians 5:7) and may every step we take be a faith step trusting that You will not allow us to stumble or fall. Your word declares to us that you will give your angels charge over our lives. If we trust You continually and even when we fall short (because it will happen) God You are still faithful. The examples of faith we see in the Bible are not that of perfect faith but of struggling faith. Many times our faith will be tested. God wants us to have a faith that will hold up even under the greatest pressure. James 1:2-4(NLT) reads "Dear brothers and sisters, when troubles of any kind come your way, consider it an opportunity for great joy. For you know that when your faith is tested, your endurance has a chance to grow. So let it grow, for when your endurance is fully developed, you will be perfect and complete, needing nothing." Where would our faith be without a test? In the same way we are given exams in school to assess what we have learned; our Heavenly Father allows tests and trials to come our way to give us an evaluation of our faith. God already knows where our faith is, we need to know where we are and how far we have come. With every round our faith grows higher and higher and when our endurance is fully developed, we won't need anything. Our tested faith allows our endurance to grow. To endure means to be able to suffer (something painful or difficult) patiently. God tells us in Romans 3:3-4 that even though we may lack faith or are even faithless He remains faithful. We can always depend on God to be the same regardless of where we are. Our failures can never cancel out God faithfulness.

Faithfulness, as we read in Galatians 5:22 is one of the fruits of the Spirit. Everything we need to live a glorious life in God has already been planted in us through His Holy Spirit. "But the Holy Spirit produces this kind of fruit in our lives: love, joy, peace, patience, kindness, goodness, faithfulness, gentleness and self-control" (NLT). The "seeds" of the fruit of the Spirit that are instilled in us need to grow. It is in the testing that not only will our faith begin to grow but our peace, joy, patience, kindness, goodness, gentleness, self-control and love will begin to blossom as well.

In Ephesians 6:13-17 we see many garments that we should be dressed in. Among these articles of clothing is the shield of faith. All of these pieces of armor are available, but we have to actively put them on or take them up! Taking up the shield of faith means that we must receive what God is so graciously willing to give. A shield can be used both offensively and defensive. Naturally the shield was used to protect the soldier. The dictionary defines a shield as a broad piece of metal, or another suitable material used as protection against blows or missiles; a person or thing providing protection. In verse 16 we see that the spiritual shield that we must take up is that of faith. It is a symbol of full protection. The word used here for shield in Greek is related to the Greek word for "door". It refers to the large 4'x2' full body shield used during biblical times. This shield was often times soaked in water to extinguish fiery arrows shot from the enemy. How can this "shield of faith" be used to extinguish these fiery darts? When the evil one hurls lies, the "fiery darts," at us we have a shield of protection. We have the Word of God and the promises of God to obliterate the lies of the devil. There were many times I did not take up my shield and I was wounded by the lies of the enemy. I believed the lies that attacked my identity I wasn't good enough, I'm not worthy. Lies that attacked my future I'll never get through this problem, no one cares if you're around. The lies that attacked my authority it's impossible, that can't be done, no one is listening to you. Yet God is still faithful even when we are not. He stands before me, His angels fight on my behalf. When my head is hung low, God is the lifter of my head. My Daddy (God, Father God, or Abba Father) reminds me that I have a defense. I don't have to idly sit by and allow myself to be pummeled by the deceptive words of the evil one. I will boldly activate my faith, grab my shield and get back in the fight! The victory is already won, we just have to stand firm.

When we truly understand the glorious gift God has given us, namely faith, we begin to look at life afresh. We begin to walk differently, knowing that the mighty God we serve leads us. We begin to talk differently, knowing our Savior speaks through us. We begin to think differently, knowing that the Almighty God has given us the ultimate victory in all things. We treat others differently, knowing our Omnipotent God is in complete control.

WHO AM I?

"But you are a chosen people, a royal priesthood, a holy nation, God's special possession, that you may declare the praises of him who called you out of darkness into his wonderful light."

1 Peter 2:9 NIV

So often we go through life not fully understanding the answer to the question, who am I? We may have some ideas of who we are. Many ideas come from our ancestry, personalities, and heritage but only through the word of God are we able to truly understand who we are. The Word of God gives us a clear picture of who we are. The world on the other hand tries (but fails) to make us into something or someone else contrary to the Word of God. We were not fashioned by the Hands of God and in the image of God to be clones (one like everyone else). We are created in the image of God with our own specific uniqueness. I believe in order to truly understand who we are we must understand our Creator in whose image we are created. Gods purpose for us was determined long before we even came into being. God already knew the purpose we would serve here on the Earth before we were in our mother's womb (Jeremiah 1:5) . It is so important to know who we are in this season if not it will be easy for us to fall for the schemes of the enemy.

First we must understand that we are created in the very image of God (Genesis 1:27-28, 2:7). These verses describe how we are created in Gods image and how God Himself formed us from the dust of the earth in His hands and blew into our lifeless bodies the powerful breath of God; the breath of life (nesh-aw-maw'/Strong's 5397 (a puff; a vital breath; divine inspiration; intellect; inspiration; the soul and the spirit). God packed so much into us with that one breath. We should not take for granted the breath God breathed into us. What are we doing with the breath God breathed into us? Are we being fruitful and multiplying? After this breath we became living souls. We were only dust from the ground in the hands of God until He breathed Life into us. God so lovingly formed us in His hands and if we allow, He will continue holding us, molding us, and shaping us in His hands. God also gave us the authority to reign to be a good stewards over the things in the earth. What exactly does it mean to be "made in His image"? The Hebrew word used for image is (tseh'-lem/Strong's 6754) meaning to shade; a phantom, i.e. (figuratively) illusion, resemblance; hence, a representative figure, especially an idol: image, vain shew. God is a Triune being (three yet One). God the Father, God the Son (Jesus), and God the Spirit (Holy Spirit). Just like God we are also three in one, triune beings. We have a spirit, a soul (mind, will, and emotion) and we live in a body. In 1 Thessalonians 5:23 Paul asks the God of Peace to sanctify us in every way and that our bodies, soul and whole spirit be kept blameless until the Lord Jesus returns. God has made us to be stewards over His creation not owners. "The earth is the Lord's, and everything in it. The world and all its people belong to him" (Psalms 24:1 NLT). We along with all of God's creation belong to Him. Proverbs 3:5 says that we must acknowledge God in all of our ways. Why? We must acknowledge Him because we belong to Him and He knows exactly where we should be going and what we should be doing. God gave the command to reign over all of His creation and He also commanded that we be fruitful and multiply. The word here in Genesis 1:28 for fruitful (paw-raw'/Strong's 6509) means to bear fruit (literally or figuratively): bear, bring forth (fruit), (be, cause to be, make) fruitful, grow, increase. Galatians 5:22 calls us to bear the fruit of the Spirit-love, joy, peace, kindness, faithfulness, gentleness, goodness, patience, and self-control. God has given us everything that pertains to life (2 Peter 1:3). Once by grace through faith we received Jesus Christ as our Savior and we now have the power to line up with the very nature of God.

We must know that we are God's great design. Jehovah God, Elohim is our creator. God has already shown us in Genesis 1:27, 2:7 that we were created in His very image and filled with His breath-the Breath in our lungs. Can you imagine that every time you speak, you are using the Breath of God? Atmospheres are changed by our mere words. This is why Psalms 150 commands that everything that has Breath PRAISE THE LORD! What exactly does it mean to be "made in the image" of God? So much of who we are is tied into who He is and who He created us to be. Psalms 139 says that He knew us before we were in our mothers' wombs. That every day of our lives was written in His book before our first day began. What assurance we should have knowing that God Almighty knows our name. God loves us so much that in Psalms 8:5 it says that we were created a little lower than the Elohim (Angels).

Who am I? What makes me so special that you would consider me? This is a question many of us have. It's amazing how easy it is to see the value and beauty in others and not in ourselves. Let us take time to look in the mirror. Use this time to write down who you are. Be honest in describing what you see inside. Good or bad what do you see when you look in the mirror? The Word of God is the most accurate mirror we will ever look into. The Word of God (the Logos) gives us a clear description of who we are. Take a look at your list. Can you identify yourself in the Word of God? If not, that's okay for now is a good time to acknowledge that we are not reflecting the image God has created us to be. Let us pray and ask the Holy Spirit to help! God's desire is that we are not conformed to this world, but we are to be transformed by the renewing of our minds (Romans 12:2). God our Father wants to display His greatness to all the earth and He wants to do it through us.

Along with knowing who we are is recognizing the authority we have in the earth (Genesis 1:28). God commands His creation (male and female) to be fruitful and multiply. To fill the earth and govern it. I love how the Amplified

Bible translates this verse "And God blessed them [granting them certain authority] and said to them, "Be fruitful, multiply, and fill the earth, and subjugate it [putting it under your power]; and rule over (dominate) the fish of the sea, the birds of the air, and every living thing that moves upon the earth" (AMP). In blessing them, God guaranteed them the authority to rule over everything in this earth where Satan and his angles were sent. This great authority, relinquished by Adam in the garden with the serpent, was redeemed by our Great Redeemer, Jesus when He gave Himself as a sacrifice for the world. Jesus in turn gives us this authority (Luke 10:19). Psalms 139 tells us more about ourselves as God's great creation. It tells us how we are known by The Most High. In this psalm David describes how wonderfully complex we are created. God tells us how we display His awesome workmanship. You made all the delicate, inner parts of my body and knit me together in my mother's womb. Thank you for making me so wonderfully complex! Your workmanship is marvelous—how well I know it. You watched me as I was being formed in utter seclusion, as I was woven together in the dark of the womb. You saw me before I was born. Every day of my life was recorded in your book. Every moment was laid out before a single day had passed. How precious are your thoughts about me, O God? They cannot be numbered! (Psalms 139:13-17 NLT)

God has given us so much ability. When we look at the gifts inside, Moses is a great example of not understanding of who he was and what he possessed. Looking at Exodus 3 and 4 we see how God uses His encounter with Moses to give us some insight in what He is also saying to us. God drew Moses in and got his attention with the burning bush. He may not get our attention as dramatic as a burning bush but it may be something else like a life test or a difficult situation. The purpose of the attention grabber is to draw us to come nearer to Him. The moment Moses was intrigued by the bush that was burning but not consumed God spoke and Moses was in a place to hear. It's amazing how clearly we can hear the voice of God when we draw close to Him. It's by drawing near that we are able to hear our call, know our purpose, and even know who we are! God's desire is for us to know Him. God wants relationship with His creation. The only true way to know who we are is to know and understand the One in whose image we were created in. God called Moses by name. God knew him! The moment Moses was drawn closer to God, God taught Moses about His holiness and how to reverence Him. God tells him to remove his sandals for he is standing on Holy Ground.

This is the same example we see as Jesus drew the Samaritan woman at the well with the living water. Once she desired the "living water" that Jesus offered He revealed the sin that separated them. Jesus prayed that we would be one as He and the Father are one. To get close to our Creator we must acknowledge the sin that separates us but all glory to God that Jesus came, suffered, died and rose from the grave to cleanse us from our sin. In verse 11 of Exodus 3 there are many emotions, fear being the most prevalent, that Moses experienced as God began to explain how He has heard the cry of His people back in Egypt. God still hears the cry of His people and He desires that we all be free. One of the first questions Moses asks God is "Who am I?" (Exodus 3:11) Moses did not consider himself qualified for the job of freeing the Israelites and besides he had tried it before and ended up running for his life. The problem with this was the first time Moses attempted to deliver his people with his own power and by his own plan. God reminds Moses and us that He is the God who is more than enough. We have to follow His lead in His time.

The second question from Moses was "What will others think of me?" God has equipped us, His great creation, with many gifts and talents. What are we doing with what we have been given? We can't compare ourselves to others because God has given to us according to our abilities. It's important that we learn to be content in what God has given us and be zealous for what He has given us. God has given us all talents that include our time, ability and money. Are we being good stewards over what God has given us? We will have to give an account of what we have done with that which God has made us stewards. There is so much God wants to do through us for His glory. God loves to yoke His anointing with the talent He has given us in order to showcase His Glory. When we look at the parable of the talents in Matthew 25:13-30 we see how important it is to use what God has given us. The story begins with a man giving "talents" or money to his servants before he embarked on a long journey. The talents were distributed according to their abilities. This is why it is so important to not compare what we have with what others have. We must trust God knows what our abilities are-He did create us and He knows the purpose He placed in us. The first two servants began immediately working to use what was given to them. However, the third servant purposed in his heart that he would hide what was given to him. Perhaps he thought maybe if the master never returns, he would at least keep what was given, maybe it was truly fear or plain laziness. What are you doing with the gifts, talents, and abilities God has entrusted you with? Are you like the two servants that went away immediately to work when they saw the value of what was given to them? Or are you like the third servant who was both wicked and lazy? If you find yourself not using what God has given you or you don't appreciate the value of your talent, it is not too late. Our Heavenly Father has not yet returned but be sure He is on his way back. Get to work while it is yet day for when the night comes no man will be able to work!

One of the gifts God has given us is authority. What is authority and why do I have it? This is a question many of us may have. One definition for authority is the power or right to give orders, make decisions, and enforce obedience, inherent (existing in something as a permanent, essential or characteristic attribute; something you get that you did not have to work for) right. Do we know who we are? We don't exercise the authority God has given us because we may not know what we possess. What we already have in our hands. Some may know the power God has given us, but we are not using it. The enemies' job is to keep us blind and ignorant of the tools God has given to us to use in this world. Many times, the Apostle Paul says that he would not have us to be ignorant in so many situations like the mysterious sovereignty of God or regarding our spiritual gifts. The Greek word used for ignorant is ag-no-eh'-o/Strong's NT 50 which means not to know through lack of information or intelligence, not know, not understand, or unknown. God has graciously provided everything we need to live an abundant life. It is ours for the asking. If we need wisdom all we need to do is ask (James 1:5). "Look, I have given you authority/power (ex-oo-see'-ah/ Strong's 1849) over all the power (doo'-nam-is/Strong's 1411) of the enemy, and you can walk among snakes and scorpions and crush them. Nothing will injure you" Luke 10:19 NLT. In this verse, we see that the first power is accompanied with authority and the second power word is just power. The enemy may have power, but it does not compare to the power and authority God has given to us. The power of life and death is in the tongue (Proverbs 18:21) and I refuse to let my current circumstance affect what comes out of my mouth. The enemy does not want us to operate in our God given authority or he wants to deceive us to use the authority God has given us against ourselves. We have the authority to operate and use the "keys" God have given us. Keys to grant access but also to refuse access. Through Jesus we now have access to the Father where we can come boldly to His throne (Ephesians 2:18, 3:12). Jesus, the one who is Holy and True, holds the key of David and what He opens no one can close and what He closes no one can open (Revelation 3:7). This is the wonderful gift God has given us, the privilege to bind and loose (see Matthew 16:19). The Kingdom keys God has bestowed to us can cause things to start and stop as well. We have the power to stop distractions or halt the works of the enemy. We can also ignite our faith or build up ourselves by prayer. This authority is in our mouths. The Word lets us know that both life and death are in the power of our tongues (Proverbs 18:21). We even have access to use the wonderful name of Jesus to perform many miracles, bringing glory to God (Mark 9:38) (Philippians 2:9-10). Yes, we have the authority to move mountains out of our way even as God gives us direction for this inherent right.

The great commission as read in Matthew 28:18 gives us a charge to go make disciples (believers in Jesus that seeks to follow Him), baptizing in the name of The Father, Son, and Holy Spirit, and to teach others the commands of God (Love the Father and love others as ourselves). We have to first go out and do the work with the gifts God has given us. Jesus tells us in John 14:12 that because of our faith in Him we will do the same works and even greater works so that God is glorified. Our work begins outside the four walls of the church building. There is so much work to be done. Making disciples is different from just encouraging others to believe (to evangelize). So many have declared the repentance prayer but have done nothing else. We have to go further than just our confession and we have to draw close to God. It is imperative that we teach others the commands of God and help to restore others in love (2 Timothy 2:2). We should want others to come and join into the fellowship. Some that we may minister to may not be physically able to come to church to worship or they may not feel comfortable. We have to love people where they are just as God loves us. This authority God has given us is for Gods glory not for our gain. In Isaiah 22:22 we read how God dealt with Shebna the wicked scribe of King Hezekiah. He sought to exalt himself by building himself a tomb among royalty. He used his authority as the king's chief officer for his own personal gain. Through the prophet Isaiah, God condemned Shebna and exalted Eliakim, who was over the kings household, giving him the keys of David. It's time that we receive the authority God has given us and use it for the glory of God.

Plot of Satan

The plot of Satan is to bring about separation, convince us that we are something we are not and to distract us. The enemy speaks lies all the time about who we are and what we possess. In Daniel 1 we read the account of when King Nebuchadnezzar conquered and enslaved some of the people from the kingdom of Judah. As we read these passages in Daniel we see several things. First, out of those he captured the King desired only the nobles and the best looking out of the bunch from Judah. He then separated them by placing them under the eyes of his leadership. The kings' servants go on to change their names to that of the gods in the land. Many times, it was to bring remembrance to their pagan gods instead of their original names that represented their Godly heritage. A lot of significance was placed when it came to naming a child in the Hebrew customs. It was either a trait they saw in their child or a quality they desired to see in them. I am sure they also put a lot of thought and prayer into naming their children. When the Babylonians gave names to the captives it was a sign of them being under their subjection (being under their control). The enemy's plot is to keep you in the dark of who you are and instead give you "fool's gold" (something that looks valuable but has no worth at all). Not only were they taken captive and striped from the land God gave them but to be renamed after the

Babylonian gods was demeaning. Daniel's name meaning "God is my judge" was changed to Belteshazzar which is translated to "Preserve thou his life". In this strategic name change, the king wanted them to know that he was the one who preserved their lives. King Nebuchadnezzar did not know or understand the power of The Almighty God, at least not yet! Daniel's name was a reminder that only God is his judge. I believe Daniel and his companions held fast to all they knew about God and everything God said about them. This is how Daniel was able to make the request to the king's servant to allow him and his friends to not defile themselves by eating the kings' food. This practice is commonly known as the "Daniel fast" that we often undertake today. Hananiah whose name means "Jah (Jehovah) has favored" was changed to Shadrach meaning "command of Aku" (moon god). Mishael whose name means "one who is like God" was changed to what we know as Meshach. One of the possible meanings of Meshach is "Who is as Aku?" Aku was the Babylonian idol, for the moon god. Lastly, Azariah whose name means "Jah (Jehovah) has helped" was changed to Abednego meaning "servant of Nego" (the god of science and literature). So many times, the enemy tries to change our name and who we are by enticing us to lean on our own understanding with our trivial shallow knowledge but God directs us in Proverbs 3:5-6 to trust in Him always and lean not to our own understanding.

King Nebuchadnezzar wanted to change everything about them to make them conform to the world even down to what they ate and drank. However, Daniel determined not to defile the laws of God and petitioned to be allowed to eat and drink what was acceptable before the Lord. In this situation God favored Daniel and his friends giving them favor with the eunuch in charge of them. The enemy has a way of making things look innocent and appetizing to the eye. Who wouldn't want to be in the kings' palace eating nothing but the best but scriptures tell us that even a little leaven destroys the lump! We cannot compromise with sin. Daniel purposed in his heart and it did not matter that he was in a high position or amongst kings because he recognized that he was a servant of the Kings of Kings. They all continued to face many tests and obstacles like we will in this life. We may not be faced with a fiery furnace or a lion's den but the consequences are the same. The effect of an unrepentant heart is the righteous anger of God (Romans 2:5). We must stand for what is right no matter the outcome just as Daniel, Hananiah, Mishael, Azariah and so many others did. The word of the Lord lets us know difficult times are coming in 2 Timothy 3:1-7 however we have a choice whether to follow after the customs of man or uphold the righteous standards of the Most High God.

In the Word of God, we see so many examples of how the enemy tries to defeat the children of God through many schemes and deceit. If we are to truly know who we are, we must search the Word of God, ask the Father to show you who we are and then confidently walk in it. What is distracting you? Get started!

RELATIONSHIP
AND INTIMACY

"O God, You are my God; with deepest longing I will seek You; My soul [my life, my very self] thirsts for You, my flesh longs and sighs for You, In a dry and weary land where there is no water. So I have gazed upon You in the sanctuary, To see Your power and Your glory. Because Your lovingkindness is better than life, My lips shall praise You. So will I bless You as long as I live; I will lift up my hands in Your name."

Psalms 63:1-4 AMP

The word relationship has many relatable examples. We have relationships with our family and with our friends. We can also have professional relationships in our workplace or ministry. However, our relationship with God, our creator, is the most important relationship of all. It is the foundation to every other relationship we will have including the relationship we have with ourselves. What does God say about our relationship with Him? God created us to have relationships. In Genesis 2:18 we see God saying it is not good for man to be alone. In the midst of this beautiful oasis filled with many "good" things God recognized that these things were not like man. God wanted His creation to understand one of the aspects of His character. God is relationship.

We see in John 1 "In the beginning the Word already existed. The Word was with God, and the Word was God". I don't know if I will ever fully understand the intimate relationship of God the Father, God the Son, and God the Spirit; however, they are three yet one.

The Word of God gives us many examples of relationships. Jesus prays in John 17 that we become one as They are one. Here Jesus wants us to experience the same glorious relationship He has with the Father "As you are in me and I am in You". Before we look at some of these examples we want to define some words. What is intimacy? What is relationship? The dictionary (dictionary.com) gives us these definitions. Intimacy is the state of being intimate. A close, familiar, and usually affectionate or loving personal relationship with another person or group; a close association with or detailed knowledge or deep understanding of a place, subject, period of history, etc. Relationship is a connection, association, or involvement or connection between persons by blood or marriage. It can also be an emotional or other connection between people.

Knowing this, let us now take a closer look into the Word of God at some of these examples. One of our first examples is Enoch. In the book of Genesis, we are not given much information about him. We are told that he walked with God. The specific details of the relationship between God and Enoch are not written but we do know that Enoch was in close intimate fellowship with God. We read in Genesis 5 that Enoch walked in close fellowship for 300 years with God. I've gone on many walks both alone and with others. One thing I've learned is that when you walk alone you can go at your own pace and go in whatever direction you choose. However, when you walk with others there are times when you may walk a little in front or behind each other but in order to have a conversation it's good to stay at the same pace and go in the same direction so that you can hear each other clearly. When I hear "walk together" in my mind I imagine walking together in step, not too far ahead and not too far behind. In these few verses we see the true nature of their relationship. It went far beyond an ordinary relationship to that of a faithful, devoted one. To walk in step with someone it means you are familiar with the length of their stride, their pace and the direction they are headed. The connection between God and Enoch was so special that one day God took him. This is the level of intimacy God desires for all of His creation. When we spend time with Him, we are able to hear His voice and walk in step with Him.

Next, let us look at the relationship between God and Job. The book of Job begins right away giving us insight into Job's character. He is described as being a man who is blameless and upright. He was not perfect but was a man of great integrity. He was one who turned away from evil and revered God. He never cursed God even when faced with opposition from his wife and closest friends. He was dealing with his failing heath, loss of his wealth and the death of all his children. Even with all of these admirable qualities we see that God desired more intimacy with Job. In the end, Job realized that even though he loved and reverenced God there was so much more about Him that he did not know. He was close but there was still room to grow closer. Can you see yourself being like Job? Maybe you did not have to endure the level of tests and trials that Job did but God has a way of using our trials to draw us closer to Him. He wants to have a deeper, more intimate connection with us.

David was described in scripture as a man after God's heart and was called God's servant. We are able to see the highs and lows of his relationship with the Lord in many of the Psalms he penned. In Psalms 18, David sings a song of praise to God after he is rescued from his enemies and Saul. David recognized God as his shield and protection. He recognized God as his rock, strength, and his defense. He accredited God with the mighty power to save him and saw that in God there is safety. David attributed the favor on his life to the mercy of God and not to any good thing he had accomplished. In Psalms 23, David recognized that God is the great shepherd. One that will take great care of His sheep. David himself was a shepherd and he understood what it took to care for sheep. David understood the love of God, the provision of God and the care God had given to him. Even in the darkest paths, David knew that God would never leave him. David fully knew that the Lord's goodness and mercy would follow (chase after) us every day of our lives. The Message translation says, "Your beauty and love chase after me every day of my life. I'm back home in the house of GOD for the rest of my life" (Psalm 23:6 MSG). It is important to know that God did not favor David because he served Him so faithfully but because of Gods great mercy and sovereignty.

In 1 Chronicles 28 David teaches his son Solomon about intimacy with God. He told him that he will be God's son and God will be his Father. David cautioned his son to have an intimate relationship with God and to take this relationship seriously. "As for you, Solomon my son, know the God of your father [have personal knowledge of Him, be acquainted with, and understand Him; appreciate, heed, and cherish Him] and serve Him with a blameless heart and a willing mind; for the LORD searches all hearts and minds, and understands every intent and inclination of the thoughts". If you seek Him [inquiring for and of Him and requiring Him as your first and vital necessity] He will let you find Him; but if you abandon (turn away from) Him, He will reject you forever" (1 Chronicles 28:9 AMP). This is a crucial lesson for us as we develop an intimate relationship with our Heavenly Father.

After his disappointing denial of Jesus, Peter decided that he was of no use to the kingdom and decided to go back to what he knew he was good at-fishing. After a night of fishing Jesus met Peter and some of the other disciples on the beach. Three times Jesus asked Peter if he loved Him and to feed His sheep. Twice Jesus asked Peter if he Agape (Strong's nt. 25) loved Him, meaning an unconditional love, a love that never waivers or fails. The third time Jesus asked if he loved (Phileo) Him. Phileo (Strong's nt. 5368) is a love that is described as a brotherly love or love as of a friend. Peter's response was always that of Phileo. Jesus sought out a closer love relationship than Peter was ready or willing to give at this time. Later on, we see how God's unconditional love towards Peter changed his love response towards Jesus (John 21:15-17).

Initially, Peter underestimated the power of the enemy and did not follow the example of Jesus spending time in prayer, in the face of God. Peter, before this encounter with the resurrected Jesus, was boastful and proud. He was humbled before the Mighty Hand of God. Peter, after the confrontation in the

Gethsemane garden, followed Jesus at a distance and not in His shadow, which would have indicated a close relationship. He found himself sitting in the midst of nonbelievers and ultimately found himself behaving like a nonbeliever-denying the One he loved. The One who loved him still. Jesus loves us so much that He gives us wonderful grace and loves us back into fellowship with Him. Even when we mess up Jesus is there waiting to love us. God is the Good Father watching for us to return and runs out to meet us, wraps His loving arms around us, and gives us a grand reception just like the good father in the parable of the prodigal son. God's love is never dependent on our reciprocated love to Him. God is love (1 John 4:8b) and He cannot change and deny who He is. However, we will experience His love greater when it is mutual, close, and intimate.

John often referred to himself as the disciple that Jesus loved most. John understood one thing that most of us apparently do not. John understood the grace and the unfailing love of God. He knew that he was not worthy of God's love but he received it. He relished in the love of God through Jesus. He understood the limitless love of God towards His children, those who follow hard after Him. I'm so glad that God has no favorites. What He does for one He is willing to do for us all. The only thing we need to do is to receive everything God wants to give us. John understood the authority in his mouth. When he called himself the disciple whom God loved, he connected with how he was viewed by God. It's a part of intimacy that we will begin to see what God sees. The more time we spend in the face of God the more we will understand how precious we are to Him. That identity will be imbedded in our hearts and we will believe it and then we will walk in it.

Jesus is the quintessential example of intimacy with the Father. Jesus explains in John 5:19 that he only does what He sees the Father doing and that there is nothing He can do on His own. This statement lets us know that Jesus was in constant communication with the Father. This also lets us know that Jesus did not have His own interest or agenda. Many times in scripture we see Jesus going away to spend time alone with God. It's in those quiet times with our Father that we can be refreshed, renewed and filled. When there is a lot of noise it is sometimes hard to clearly hear the voice of God; however, when we have sweet communion with the Holy Spirit He makes everything so clear.

Jesus has set the precedent of how our relationship should look with God our Father. It is a relationship that consists of close and constant communication, surrender and obedience. Being fully aware of the love God has for Him, Jesus walked confidently in His authority. This is the same love God has for us. In everything, Jesus made sure to give all of the glory to God. Every blinded eye that was opened, every person raised from the dead, every miraculous provision Jesus made sure that He pointed them to His Heavenly Father, our Father.

God knows where we are and He knows the depths of our relationship with Him. God desires for us to follow close to Him in order to strengthen our relationship with Him and to have an intimate relationship with Him. He wants us to go from merely a head knowledge to a heart knowledge. There is a difference between knowing about someone and then to know someone and all the small details of their life . I remember a time when I worked as a clinical specialist traveling to different states providing education. There were many of us who traveled together and there were times when I was with other clinical specialists I'd worked with in the past and other times when it was an initial introduction. On one particular occasion I met a new person and we learned that we shared a mutual friend, Julie (not her real name). I excitedly replied, yes I know Julie we've work together for many years. Well, as it would turn out my new found friend let Julie know that she'd met me and we were now working together. Julie let her promptly know that I couldn't know her because she did not know me at all. I was so devastated and embarrassed. I fell into the trap so many of us do. I assumed that we knew each other. Why not we were on so many shared emails. We were at some of the same personal events. I had knowledge of her family. How could she say I didn't know her? After I recovered from the damaging blow to my pride, I realized she was right. Though I knew a lot about her and we worked for the same company for many years, we never had a face to face conversation. We were never formally introduced. This encounter made me realize that there are so many who know about Jesus. They may have heard the blessed stories from their mothers, fathers, grandparents or friends but never experienced a personal introduction themselves. Maybe you have been introduced and that's where it ended. There was no further relationship building. When my life is over, I want to hear Jesus say, "well done my good and faithful servant" not "depart from me because I never knew you".

Our experience with God can be so much greater when we do things as God intends. Now we must evaluate our own relationship with God. Jesus prayed in John 17 that we become one (in perfect unity) as He and the Father are one. This is, I believe, the gold standard. The one we should emulate. When we look at one of my favorite scriptures, Psalms 91, it says that the one who stays in the shelter of the Most High will find rest in the shadow of the Almighty. It is a blessed place to be in the shadow of God. In His shadow we find rest, security, protection, provision, and most importantly we see where He is leading us. We must stay close to our Creator in order to walk in His shadow. To be in constant communication with God, to stay in His glorious presence and stay in His shadow. This does not mean that we will never encounter opposition from the enemy but when faced with difficult times we are assured that we are never alone. God is always with. Even when we may not be where we should be in our relationship with God He is always there. Let us seek the Lord and His strength. God wants us to seek His face continually (1 Chronicles 16:11). When we possess this intimate relationship with Abba we will have a greater confidence in our walk through this life. Performing all that God intends for us.

PRAYER AND FASTING

"But when you pray, go away by yourself, shut the door behind you, and pray to your Father in private. Then your Father, who sees everything, will reward you."

"But when you fast, comb your hair and wash your face. Then no one will notice that you are fasting, except your Father, who knows what you do in private. And your Father, who sees everything, will reward you."

Matthew 6:6, 17-18 NLT

Prayer is an intimate conversation with God. Fasting is defined as voluntarily going without food in order to focus on prayer and fellowship with God. Prayer and fasting often go hand in hand but may not always be the case. We can definitely pray without fasting, but we cannot fast without prayer and consecration. Pray without fasting is permissible but when we combine them together, we draw closer to our Father and begin to fully experience the Glorious presence of God. Having a dedicated time of prayer and fasting is not a way to manipulate God into doing what we desire however it is a way to really focus on God for His strength, provision, and wisdom that we so desperately need.

In the midst of our fast we must be mindful to consecrate ourselves to God. What does it mean to consecrate? To consecrate or consecration means to wholly dedicate yourself to something of greatest importance. When spoken plainly, consecration refers to the act of setting yourself aside and dedicating yourself to a deity, and that deity almost always refers to the God of Christianity (dictionary.com). Moreover, sanctification means to make holy; set apart as sacred; consecrate; to purify or free from sin(dictionary.com). In Exodus 19:10 God called on Moses to let the people know that they needed to prepare themselves to commune with the Lord Himself. They needed to wash their clothes and Moses was to sanctify them. The children of Israel needed to be ready to be in the presence of the King! Ultimately, the purpose for fasting is to "kill" the flesh. No longer our will but God's will be done. Anything we continue to feed not just physically but also spiritually will live and thrive.

We will be discussing some of the key points of both prayer and fasting but this is not all inclusive. Prayer, as we previously discussed, is an intimate communication with the Father and more importantly it should be a two-way conversation. Colossians 4 encourages us to devote ourselves to prayer with an alert mind and a thankful heart. Prayer can and should be done both secretly and among others. We should not be ashamed of having a relationship with our Heavenly Father. Praying corporately with our fellow brethren is also very important. In Luke 2:36 we are introduced to a prophet named Ana. She was a widow from the tribe of Asher. The Word tells us that after her husband died she never left the temple of God but instead stayed there worshiping God with fasting and prayer. Ana abided in the presence of God and because of this she was ready and in position when God needed her.

This is an example to us of what our posture should look like. We are not told what type of fast she did, whether it was a complete fast or a fast from sunup to sundown, but we do know that she consecrated herself because she stayed in the temple. We have to stay in communion with God in order to always be ready when He calls on us. This call on us could be to speak or be silent, it may be to intercede privately for others in prayer or prophecy publicly. Regardless of the call we must be prepared.

In 1 Thessalonians 5:7 we are told to pray without ceasing. We should always be either speaking or listening to our God. Prayer should be our lifestyle. The enemy seeks to distract us from accomplishing the work God has commissioned us to do. However, when we make prayer our lifestyle the distractions may come but they will not detour us from our purpose. Paul, an apostle of Jesus, was fully aware that prayer was a very important part of his ministry. Paul's prayers included thanking God for his fellow believers (Philippians 1:3-4, Romans 1:8-10) or praying for the salvation of others (Romans 10:1). Paul also prayed that Gods name would be glorified in us (1 Thessalonians 3:13) and that our hearts, in the midst of the trials we may face, be encouraged (Romans 15:13). One of the most important prayers Paul prayed is when he pointed believers to Jesus by encouraging them to pray for themselves (Colossians 4:2-4, Romans 15:30).

In addition to spending time making petitions to our Father, prayers should be a time of worship expressing our love and gratefulness to God. You can pray the prayer of salvation or we can pray when we need to receive the comfort only God can give. There are prayers when we are seeking guidance and we should always seek His guidance. There are also prayers regarding healing for either ourselves or others. It can be a physical, spiritual or mental healing that needs to take place. James 5:13-16 calls for prayers of intercession (coming on behalf of someone else). Moses interceded on the behalf of his sister Miriam when she was stricken with leprosy. God heard his cry and she was healed. We should be praying and thanking God for the many blessings He continually showers upon us and we definitely need prayer in times of weakness. Constant and consistent prayer is necessary because in our own power we can do nothing. It is by His grace, mercy and power that we can do all things. Our prayers should be fervent which means to be resolute in our petitions and we should press into prayer. When we pray, we should do so expecting to hear from our Father. Psalms 5:3 says that I bring my requests to you each morning and wait expectantly. When we pray we enter into the realm of the Spirit. Revelation 8:4

speaks to how powerful our prayers are. Here we read as the angel of the Lord is at the altar in Heaven. He was given the smoke of the incense to mix with the prayers of the saints. We have also read many times in Old Testament scripture how the sacrifice placed on the altar was a sweet aroma to the Lord. Jesus was the perfect sacrifice and His surrendered death on the cross was pleasing to the Father (Ephesians 5:2).

Again in Revelations 8:4, the angel of the Lord filled the incense burner with the fire from the altar and threw it to the earth. God is affected by our prayers and His response is always earth shattering! He is ready to move the mountains in our lives. He is prepared to destroy every stronghold the enemy has setup in our minds. Our prayers have power. Satan (the great deceiver) does not want us to connect with our Father in the spiritual realm. This is where we find peace, where we gain our strength, get divine direction and receive refreshing. Satan's desire is that we stay frustrated, weak, lost and dry. When we are spiritually dry we don't even want to seek God much less spend time with Him. In these times we definitely have to press harder knowing that our Father is always listening and answering our prayers. It pleases the Father to bring you peace, strength, guidance and refreshing.

In Matthew 6:5 Jesus discusses in what manner we should both pray and fast. The first word in verse 5 is "when". This shows me that prayer is not and should not be considered optional. We should develop a relationship with our Father/Creator that is personal (in private) and prayer is that relationship builder. The more time we spend in prayer the closer and stronger our relationship with our Creator will become.

"When you pray, don't be like the hypocrites who love to pray publicly on street corners and in the synagogues where everyone can see them. I tell you the truth, that is all the reward they will ever get. But when you pray, go away by yourself, shut the door behind you, and pray to your Father in private. Then your Father, who sees everything, will reward you. When you pray, don't babble on and on as the Gentiles do. They think their prayers are answered merely by repeating their words again and again. Don't be like them, for your Father knows exactly what you need even before you ask him!" (Matthew 6:5-8) When praying

we should make it private and conversational as we develop our personal relationship with our Creator.

In the "Lords Prayer" or model prayer found in Matthew 6:9 and Luke 11:2-4 Jesus shows us a better way. The "model prayer" or as some call it the "Apostles' prayer" is the prayer that Jesus gave to the disciples when they asked Him to teach them how to pray. Jesus gave them an outline of the way to make our petitions to the Lord. We can pray this prayer word for word and God will honor His word. More so, I believe it to be a model on how to pray. Let's look into the scriptures. First, we see in Matthew 6:9 NLT "Our Father in heaven may your name be kept holy". This is to acknowledge who we are talking to and the nature of our relationship. God is our Father. He is our creator. We are coming to talk with our Daddy! We also recognize that His throne is in heaven. We confess His majesty and His holiness. The very name of God (Jehovah, Yah) is Holy. We should not dishonor His name. The name of the Lord should be held in high esteem. Matthew 6:10 NLT "May your kingdom come soon. May your will be done on earth, as it is in heaven". The word for kingdom here in the original Greek is βασιλεία (Strong's NT 932) {bas-il-i'-ah} from βασιλεύς; properly, royalty, i.e., (abstractly) rule, or (concretely) a realm (literally or figuratively): kingdom, + reign. Here is a call for God's capacity as Lord and King to control Earth like He does Heaven. We are Earth! This is a declaration that we desire God to not only reign over us but also to reign in our lives. The day we received Jesus as our Lord a savior we died to this world and the things of this world. Romans 6 reminds us that sin no longer is our master and we are now dead to its power in our lives. We have a new life since we are made alive in Christ. We are born again.

Matthew 6:11 NLT "Give us today the food we need." While this verse can mean Gods provision of the physical food we need, it is also a plea for the spiritual food we will need for each day. The Word tells us that His mercies are new every morning in Lamentations 3:23. Our Father knows everything we will encounter each day, but it is up to us to pray and thank God for giving us what we need this day (today). Matthew 6:12 NLT "Forgive our sins (debts) as we forgive others who sin (are indebted) against us." If we read further down, we will see in verse 14 that God cannot forgive us if we don't forgive others. We have to show the same grace given to others that God gives us (Colossians 3:13). This is sometimes a difficult thing to do but it is necessary so that we can experience the fullness of Gods blessings in our lives. Forgiveness heals us. It heals us from anger, bitterness, rage and allows us to put on mercy, kindness, humility, gentleness, patience and love.

Matthew 6:13 NLT says, "Don't let us yield to temptation but rescue us from the evil one." It does not say that temptation will not come but that He will help us not give into the sin that temptation can bring. James 1:12 NLT says, "God blesses those who patiently endure testing and temptation. Afterward they will receive the crown of life that God has promised to those who love him." Jesus tells his disciples in Luke 22:40 to pray that they do not give into temptation. "The temptations in your life are no different from what others experience. God is faithful. He will not allow the temptation to be more than you can stand. When you are tempted, he will show you a way out so that you can endure" (1 Corinthians 10:13 NLT).

Jesus fasted and prayed in order to resist the enemy, so why do we feel like we can go through life's battles doing anything less than what was modeled for us? Jesus also refuted the enemy with the Word of God. Praying using the Scriptures is a wonderful way to remind God of what He has said about our families, our health, finances, our leaders, relationships and even our purpose in life. When Jesus endured temptation in the wilderness, He debunked the lies of the enemy with the all-powerful Word of God.

Praying in the Spirit is an essential and powerful weapon for the believer. What exactly does this mean? The Word in Romans 8:26 tells us that Holy Spirit intercedes for us with moaning and groans that we cannot comprehend when we are at a loss for words to pray. God knows exactly what we need. He is there to bring us comfort, peace and an answer to our prayers. Prayer, namely praying in the Spirit, is a vital piece of armor along with the other spiritual weapons listed in Ephesians 6:18. We must be alert and conscience of our prayers and we must be specific in our prayers. I believe when we surrender and allow Holy Spirit to take control when we pray, we begin to pray the will of the Father and not our own will or motives. In Jude 1:20 praying in the power of the Holy Spirit means using Gods words/the breath of God that has power. When we pray using Gods word, He responds. God always responds to His Word. The promises of God are yes and amen. It is part of Gods character that He cannot lie. If He says it, it shall come to pass. This is why when we pray in the power and might of Holy Spirit atmospheres begin to change. Your situations and surroundings have no other choice but to transform for the mere fact we are using the creative, mountain moving, yoke destroying words of our God. Praying in the Spirit does not necessarily mean praying in your prayer language (tongues) as mentioned in 1 Corinthians 14:13 but it is available to those who choose to receive this spiritual gift. Using the gift of praying in tongues does not make a prayer more important or successful neither does not praying in tongues negate a prayer or make it less powerful. It is vital, however, to ask God for the gift of interpretation along with the gift of speaking in tongues so both your spiritual man and your understanding can be enlightened.

When we come together in prayer with our brothers and sister in Christ our prayers are ignited. We read in Acts 1 how 120 prayed in the upper room on one accord and the Holy Spirit came in like a mighty rushing wind. The power of Holy Spirit swept through the room and filled every believer there. As a result of the fervent prayers many that heard were able to receive salvation. Also in Acts 16 not only were Paul and Silas were thrown into prison but they were placed into the inner dungeon and their feet bound to keep them from escaping. They could have easily given up and accepted defeat; however, they prayed and praised God with the singing of hymns. Because of their fervency in prayer not only were their shackles released but the jailer and everyone else in his household was saved. It was because Paul and Silas did not look at their circumstances and fall into a pit of depression and defeat instead they looked unto God from where all of the help comes from they were able to share the love of God with others. God used them as a testimony to others and to display His glory. Just like Paul and Silas God is waiting to use you in every circumstance. Come to Him in prayer that His glory can be richly displayed in you! God is always listening (Jeremiah 29:12). The prayers of the righteous benefits not only us but those around us.

The Bible is also very clear in how we should fast, we should not fast to be seen by men or be pitied by others (Matthew 6:16). Fasting does many things in us and for us. Isaiah 58:6-14 describes some of the benefits of fasting: Every yoke is broken, we are loosed from the bands of wickedness, heavy burdens are lifted, our own faults are uncovered, our soul is satisfied, we stop speaking vanity and begin to bless others instead of seeking to please only ourselves, we will call on the Lord and receive answers our to prayers.

Who is fasting for and what does God desire from fasting? Fasting is for the believer. God gives us a clear description of fasting in Isaiah 58:6-11 that He is focused on developing and maturing our character. God wants us to mortify our flesh to kill our selfish ways and desires so that our hearts desire will be to seek His face, His Spirit, and to answer His call. Abstaining from food and/or water along with consecration should bring about a change in our character. What good is fasting if we continue to fight, gossip and cause chaos? Fasting, the denial of food and/or water is to bring our flesh into submission to the will of God. In Genesis 4:1-7 God tells Cain that he must subdue sin and be its master because sin is crouching at the door eager to control him. This is the same for us. This is not just the sin brought on through the temptations of the enemy, but also the sin that lies within our own fleshly desires. When we enter into a fast we should go in with the mindset that we are going to feed our spirit man and starve the physical man. It's the things we feed that gets stronger. There are many reasons we may consider a fast but trying to get God to do something for you is not one of them. God is good and He is a good Father. He would not withhold any good thing from you (Psalms 84:11). One may consider fasting to gain proper direction in our lives or life's circumstances. King Jehoshaphat in 2 Chronicles 20:3 led his people in fasting and prayer after the armies of the Moabites, Ammonites, and some of the Meunites declared war against them.

He began his prayer by acknowledging God and His deity. Jehoshaphat was in a desperate situation. He pleaded with God for guidance. Jehoshaphat began to remind God of His Word and His promises to His people. In the midst of the prayer and fasting by the King Jehoshaphat and all the people (men, women and children) an answer came from the Lord. The Spirit came on one of the men standing there to proclaim the Word of the Lord. In this example, we see that God came swiftly to answer the prayers of His people but sometimes we may have to wait on an answer. Jeremiah waited ten days for an answer when he prayed for guidance but he received an answer (Jeremiah 42:2-7).

We must be careful that we are not fasting and praying for God to cosign something we have already determined in our hearts. Be assured that God will always respond to His people. Psalms 5:3 says that each morning I will bring my requests and I will wait expectantly for an answer. That should be our stance. We should expect God to answer each time we pray. There have been so many times where I was in dire need of an answer but I was not willing to wait. I wanted a quick answer and sometimes I became frustrated when I did not hear an answer in my time. I have to admit, I didn't know if I was even worthy of an answer. However, He is willing and waiting for us to slow down and listen for His voice.

There will be times when we will need to seek the counsel of God concerning various circumstances we encounter along life's journey. In Esther 4:11-17 we see Queen Esther was in a very difficult position. It was not permissible for the Queen to come before the King unless she was summoned to do so. The decision to go in uninvited to speak with the King could cost her life if he does not hold out the gold scepter accepting her audience. Esther was not hasty in her decision to see the King and sought God for direction. She also petitioned others to pray and fast for her, giving them clear instructions on how to fast for her (no food or water for three days). After completing her fast, Esther boldly went before the King with full expectation that God would lead her in what to say and do. Esther was successful in her endeavor. We can find the same success if we remain faithful to Gods call for us to fast, pray and seek His Face.

It is God's desire for us to come boldly into His presence. It is through the sacrifice of Jesus that we can come boldly to God without the sentence of death. He has torn the veil that separated us from Himself and He is holding out the gold scepter for us. Let us draw near. Just like Queen Esther there may be times when we need to call on others to fast and pray with us. Fasting and prayer definitely builds our relationship with God and when done corporately brings unity in the body of Christ. The prophets and the teachers of the church fasted and worshipped the Lord when the Holy Spirit appointed Barnabas and Saul for their special work (Acts 13:2). Paul and Barnabas prayed and fasted when they turned the elders over to the care of the Lord (Acts 14:23). There are times when the church body will come together to fast and pray for something specific. There is great power when we come together and are all on one accord.

During the intimate time Moses spent with God on Mount Sinai he fasted forty days. (Deuteronomy 9:9-18) Moses spent so much time in God's presence that his entire countenance changed. (Exodus 34:29) Being in the company of God changes not only our hearts, minds and attitude but others will begin to take note of the glory of God shining in our lives and even on our faces.

There may be times of fasting when we need to repent or we need to be strengthened. After Jonah preached to the city of Nineveh everyone in the city fasted and prayed. They denounced the evil committed against God and His people. In this case the fast was an outward show of the inward sorrow they had for disappointing God. In 1 Kings 19 we read how Elijah, after defeating the prophets of Baal, was feeling depressed and lonely after Queen Jezebel threatened to kill him. Elijah was at the point of utter despair when he cried out to the Lord. God sent angels to provide Elijah with food and water prior to him being sent on a forty day journey of fasting. God escorted Elijah directly into His presence. Feelings of hopelessness and loneliness can be debilitating and going to our Heavenly Father may not be our first thought but it should be. We can give all our cares to God because he truly cares for us. When we come, crying out to God, He will refresh us.

When beginning your fast you should start by preparing your mind, heart, spirit and body. It is important to have a clear purpose for fasting and what you hope to gain from your fast. You should consult with your doctor before beginning any fast, especially if you are taking medications that require you to take food with them. Paul warns in 1 Corinthians 7:5 against refraining from sexual intimacy in a marriage unless it has been agreed on in order to give yourselves completely to prayer. Therefore, when you are married it is important to agree with your spouse on the timeframe you will be fasting. Fasting should not be just another task to check off a list of to-dos. Plan fasts during times where you can spend quality time praying and communing with your Father.

Prior to starting His public ministry Jesus embarked upon a forty day fast in order to strengthen His inner man. You may wonder how long should I fast? Prayer is definitely a key component to determine how long you should fast and what you should abstain from. Every element of the fast should be God orchestrated. When we seek His guidance He will lead us in what to abstain from and how long we should be in this position. Fasting is a time where we take the focus off of ourselves and our problems so that we can redirect our attention towards God. Most of us may not have forty days where we can devote time and still away like Jesus did but maybe we have three hours for forty days. Remember God is looking for quality time not a specific amount of time.

As a disciple of the Most High God, having a lifestyle of fasting and prayer is so important. When we spend intimate time with our Heavenly Father we are in a position to receive His love, strength, and guidance. When we stay in a posture of prayer, weapons may form but they will not prosper. Prayer and fasting opens our eyes and ears to see and hear what our Father desires for us. If you have established a life of fasting and prayer, remain in Him. If you have not, then the time is now! The Lord God wants to hear from you and more importantly He wants you to hear from Him.

THE ANATOMY
OF A SERVANT

"Don't be selfish; don't try to impress others. Be humble, thinking of others as better than yourselves. Don't look out only for your own interests, but take an interest in others, too. You must have the same attitude that Christ Jesus had."

Philippians 2:3-5 NLT

When I think about anatomy I think of the human body. Although anatomy does refer to the branch of science concerned with the bodily structure of humans, animals or other living organisms it is also the study of the structure or internal workings of something. We must study the Word to truly know who we are and understand the original intention of our creator's design. God definitely works from the inside out. Romans 6:13 says that we must use our whole body as an instrument to do what is right for the glory of God. What does God say about my spiritual anatomy? What is his design for my inner workings? What should my character look like? Being called the servant of The Most High God is both a blessing and a great responsibility. Joshua Chapter 1 begins with Moses, the servant of God, gone and now Joshua, who was at Moses' side for many years, is to take his place as leader of the Israelites. As Moses' assistant, I'm sure Joshua gained a wealth of knowledge on what it took to lead Gods people and how to follow after God by watching the leadership skills of Moses. In Joshua 1 we can truly see our God being a good Father, who wants to see us succeed because we represent His name in the Earth. Many times, Joshua was told to be strong and courageous because God knows that we are going to face encounters that try to shake us, weaken us, and attempt to invoke fear. However, God has not given us a spirit of fear but a spirit of power, love and self-control (2 Timothy 1:7). The assurance of the Lord is that no one will be able to stand against us! Oh, what a blessed assurance that is. No matter what or who comes up against us, God is with us and He is fighting for us.

God gave Joshua several other instructions on how to successfully lead His people. Along with the promise to be with him, God imparted unto Joshua (and us) to follow all of His instructions and don't deviate to the right or to the left. We must be sure to follow where He (God) leads. When we do this, we acknowledge that we trust God and trust that He knows what's best for us. God promises to never leave us or forsake us. Next, God says to be faithful in studying the book of instruction. The Word of God, the Bible, is our book of instruction. It is so important to not only know for yourself what God declares in His word but we should also be able to correctly explain the word of truth to others. The word of God is also the most common way God, our Father, is speaking to us. As a servant of God, it is important to always heed His commands. Listening to and obeying the voice of God keeps us in line and keeps us in His peace and in His plan. It's only when we listen and submit to God that we prosper in all that we do. In these verses God also cautions us (Joshua) not to be discouraged. I'm in awe of the Majesty of our God that He knows that sometimes we may experience discouragement along our walk with Him. A loss of confidence in ourselves, family, our friends or even the enthusiasm of our walk with God. Yet again God says we don't have to fret because He is right there with us. He is there to heal our broken hearts. He is there to fill the empty spaces and He is there to rekindle the fire in us that "the issues of life" may have tried to extinguish.

The thirteenth chapter of John gives us more insight into our godly nature. In this chapter, Jesus gives us a perfect blueprint of what we should look like as a servant of the Most High. In this chapter, we find Jesus and the disciples participating in the Passover meal, which we know as the Last Supper. Here Jesus gives us key characteristics of a godly servant in the kingdom. The first characteristic we see Jesus model is staying in Gods' presence. John 13:1 begins with Jesus knowing His hour had come. Jesus was fully aware of God's timing because He stayed in His presence. The Greek word used for knowing {I'-do} (Strong's nt 1492) in this verse is to be fully aware; have insight It is because Jesus stayed in constant communication with God that He was able to see and understand the plans of God.

We also have the precious gift of knowing the move of God when we choose to stay in His presence. Jesus explained in John 5:19 that He can do nothing by Himself and that He only does what He sees the Father doing. What does this mean to stay in the presence of God? It means to be steady in prayer. It also means we must read and obey the Word of God which is His voice. In addition to knowing the move of God, Psalms 16:11 declares that in the presence of God there is the fullness of joy. When we stay on the path that God has set before us we have joy and peace. This is the type of joy that is not dependent on our circumstances. Isaiah 30:21 NLT reads "Your own ears will hear him. Right behind you a voice will say, "This is the way you should go," whether to the right or to the left." God wants to show us the way to stay in His divine presence. When we get close to God, in His space, He reveals all of the things that are not pleasing to Him. We begin to be transformed into His image by the renewing of our minds. Are we willing to listen and obey? Now is the time to get close so we can clearly hear the voice of Yahweh and know the next move. Exodus 33:14 says that we find rest in His presence. It is key to stay in the presence of The Most High in order to stay under the shadow of The Almighty. This is where we find safety, peace, joy and rest! Even our Father desires that we come close in His presence. Psalms 27:8 declares I can hear in my heart God calling me and my heart responds Lord I'm coming. We were created to have connection with our Creator. Every fiber of our being long to be close. Let's draw near.

John 10:27 says that My sheep know and recognize my voice. I know them and they follow me. To know someone's voice is to have relationship with them. I think of times when I was in a crowded room and I heard my child calling out to me. I knew it was my baby. I didn't have to see them because I recognized their call and they knew my voice when I said here I am. There was no doubt in my mind that I was speaking to my child and they knew to follow the sound of my voice. This is the same for our loving Father. He is always near and He is quick to answer our call. When we stay in the presence of God, He is faithful to lead us on a righteous path.

Secondly, we see in John 13:2, that we are to guard our hearts. It says that the devil prompted Judas to betray Jesus by putting it in his heart. Part of me wonders if by heart it means his mind. Do we entertain unclean malicious thoughts in our minds and then they enter our hearts? The Greek word here (kar-dee'-ah/Strong's NT 2588) is translated thoughts or feelings (mind). So then we must be careful of the things we allow to cloud or muddle our thoughts, be careful of the things we see and even the things we listen to. The enemy is always looking for an entrance. Philippians 4:8 (NLT) admonishes us to fix your thoughts on what is true, and honorable, and right, and pure, and lovely, and admirable. Think about things that are excellent and worthy of praise. We must be careful what enters our eyes and ears because they fuel our thoughts and often times our actions. Proverbs 17:24 NLT says that sensible people keep their eyes glued on wisdom, but a fool's eyes wander to the ends of the earth.

We should keep our eyes on Jesus. We are made in the image of the All Mighty God and He is neither deaf nor blind (Psalms 94:9) and He would not have us to be either (Isaiah 35:5). Proverbs 4:23 says in the NIV "Above all else, guard your heart, for everything you do flows from it". As we read in Philippines 2:5 we should let the mind of Christ abide in us. The word "mind" (fron-eh'-o/ Strong's NT 5426) here translates from its original text as "to exercise the mind or to have an opinion". It is a process to replace our way of thinking with the way God thinks. And just like physical exercise we must practice continually in order to get stronger. Ephesians 4:23 says that we should let the Spirit renew our thoughts and attitudes. We do this by letting go of our former way of thinking and living and yielding to Holy Spirit. Jesus reminds us of this in Matthew 12:34 that whatever is in your heart will determine what comes out of your mouth. We must be cognizant of the things that enter our minds and hearts because they influence the choices we make in our lives. The "Breastplate of Righteousness" mentioned in Ephesians 6:14 is one of the pieces of armor we should always wear in this spiritual war we are engaged in. It covers and protects our hearts. This breastplate we wear is not our own righteousness but it is the righteousness of God afforded to us through the sacrifice of Jesus (2 Corinthians 5:21). We have so many feelings and not all of them tells us the truth. This is why our hearts must be covered (guarded) with truth, faith and love. When we cover our hearts with this breastplate the fiery darts that the enemy hurls at us must now go through the filter of Gods righteousness and the lies of the enemy cannot even stand up against the Word of Truth. The word of God reminds us that no weapon formed against us shall prosper and every tongue that rises against us the Lord shall condemn. We must stay alert and always be watchful (1 Thessalonians 5:8). It is time to get dressed, get into position and stand firm! The battle is already won! Isaiah 59:17 shows us how even God Himself is clothed in the armor. Why do we believe we need anything less?

Knowing who we are in Christ is the third principle we see here in John 13 and it is key. It is the difference of ownership and actually taking possession. It is possible to own something but if you never take possession of it you don't get the owners' benefits. When we truly grab hold of who we are and to whom we belong to we begin to walk and talk differently. In John 13:3 (NLT) "Jesus knew that the Father had given him authority over everything and that he had come from God and would return to God." It is because Jesus was aware of who He was that He was able to exercise His authority in the Earth. It is also why He was so willing to serve others. Jesus did not think Himself to be so high that he could not do something as demeaning and degrading as washing the feet of His disciples. He even washed the feet of the one who would betray Him. How difficult that must have been to serve and be loyal to the one destined to be disloyal to you. However, Jesus knew it is was necessary. The Word tells us to

Love our enemies, that we should bless those that may curse us and to do good to those who may even hate us (Matthew 5:44).

Jesus says in Matthew 20:28 that He didn't come to be served but instead to serve others. With Jesus knowing who He was He also knew what He was there to do. He operated in purpose and He did not allow distractions to deter Him. We also have access to that same knowledge. God wants us to know who we are and to walk in purpose. Our Heavenly Father wants us to grab hold of all the blessings He has prepared for us and put them to use. It is all for His Glory and for our good. It is time to take possession of your inheritance.

The next part of the framework of a servant of God is knowing how to take charge. Taking charge does not mean taking over. To take charge in the Kingdom of God means not being afraid or ashamed to do the things God has commissioned us to do. It means to not be slow but to be obedient and be quick about getting God's business done. "We must quickly carry out the tasks assigned us by the one who sent us. The night is coming, and then no one can work" (John 9:4 NLT). Jesus did not wait to do what He knew needed to be done and He showed so much humility taking on such a filthy task as washing someone else's feet. Especially during those times where they wore sandals and their feet were not only exposed to dirt and mud but also the excrements of all the animals around.

Jesus tells his disciples that this is an example of what they should also do. We must be willing to wash the feet of our brothers and sisters. I often wonder why the feet. Then I think about what we do with our feet.... We walk. It is our walk in this life that we must be mindful of. Others watch our walk more than just listen to what we have to say. My dear Pastor (Bishop E.L.Ellison) would always say, "I hear what you're saying but I see what you are doing". We should make sure that our talk matches up with our walk in life. The many things Jesus taught He was also a living and moving blueprint of those same things. This is how we should also be. No more "Do as I say and not as I do". We should represent our Heavenly Father well in the Earth.

The book of Galatians (6:1) commissions us to restore one another in the spirit of meekness. We must have a resolve to do the things God has commanded us to do no matter the cost. It may not be an actual physical foot washing but a washing in the spirit. We should not be put off by those with "filthy lifestyles" but instead we should be willing to get on our knees in prayer interceding for them. It is in this take charge attitude that Jesus showed His great leadership skills. Jesus established that He is a man of great integrity. He was confident in who He was and He inspired others to have the same confidence. We should all have the mind of Christ, humble and thinking of others before ourselves.

Having a surrendered spirit means to cease resistance and to submit to authority. This is yet another great attribute of a Godly servant. When we received Jesus as our Lord and Savior we declared Him Lord over our lives and affirmed He has complete rule over us. While we did immediately confess with our mouths, I believe that complete surrender transpires over time. When God awakens us to this new life He is constantly revealing in us parts of our lives where we have not allowed Him to completely reign over. As Jesus came to wash Peter's feet in John 13:6, Peter initially refused to allow Him to wash his feet. Why did Peter not want his feet to be washed by Jesus? Was it because he thought that his teacher, the one in whom he looked up to, should not be doing such a subservient act? Could it have been embarrassment of how filthy his feet were? Maybe Peter was too prideful? I know I would probably be hesitant to allow the King of Kings and Lord of Lords to wash the muck and mire off of my feet. My first inclination would be to say let me clean it up a little before I let you wash them. This is what we often do spiritually. This seems to be a very common statement that we want to get our lives "straightened out" before coming to God. We must realize we can never clean ourselves. It would be like washing dirt with dirt. Jesus says to Peter "Unless I wash you, you won't belong to me". It is the blood of Jesus that makes us clean. His blood makes us that church without spot or wrinkle. Peter, being so zealous, then wanted to be washed from head to toe. I love how the Message Bible translates Jesus' response "Jesus said, If you've had a bath in the morning, you only need your feet washed now and you're clean from head to toe. My concern, you understand, is holiness, not hygiene" (John 13:10-12

MSG). Remember that to surrender means we must completely submit to authority. In this case we are to submit ourselves to the authority of Jesus. We should not question God's motives when He instructs us to do something or even to go to various places. We have to wholly trust that God knows what He is doing and He is in full control. When we submit to the authority of Our God we fully relinquish our rights to Him. Just as Jesus cried out in the garden "not my will but Thy will be done" so we must cry out too. It is time to let go of the illusion of control we think we have in this life and allow the One who is always in control to take the wheel.

The next characteristic Jesus modeled for us in John 13 is using restraint. Imagine the self-control exercised by Jesus during this Passover meal. Not only did He wash the feet of the one who would betray Him but also showed unconditional love to Judas and fed him at the table as well. This must have been a difficult task, but it was necessary. I realize the command to love and bless those who may be against us is so different from what we see in this world but we operate under the authority of the Kingdom of God. We are to represent His Kingdom in the earth. What great reserve Jesus used to delay the announcement to His betrayer that He was fully aware of his plans. I would have probably shouted it across the room with my accusatory finger pointed directly at Judas screaming, "He's about to betray me".

James tells us that the tongue, a very small organ, is very difficult to tame. He says that if we could tame the tongue we would be perfect. Imagine that, perfection achieved by the discipline of such a small seemingly insignificant part of our bodies. The scripture goes on to let us know that the tongue is a fire and a small spark can set a forest on fire and no one can tame the tongue. Jesus knew how the events were to unfold, He was unshaken. He perfectly showed complete control. Jesus had so much more to give to His disciples and this was not the time to cause a scene. It was after Judas left to betray Jesus that Jesus gave the command to love to the other disciples. Jesus gives the disciples (and us) a mandate that we should love on another and by this love the world would know that we are His disciples. It is the way we show the Love of God that men realize that we follow hard after God.

There is a big difference between a believer and a disciple. Many people believe but only a few follow Him. In the Kingdom of God, the greatest will be the least and the least will be greatest. First shall be last and the last first. Are there areas in your life where you can learn from Jesus' example of using restraint? By the power of Holy Spirit we are able to show godly restraint. We have to understand that our words have power. Life and death are in the power of our tongues (Proverbs 18:21). We may not be perfect but as Paul says in Philippians 3 "I press towards the mark". I will keep on going, I won't stop trying until I get to Jesus.

Everything Jesus did He did it for the Glory of God. This is yet another example of what it means to be a servant of The Most High. Jesus says in John 5:19 that He does only what He sees the Father doing. Jesus is very careful to always give Glory to God. We must realize that we cannot accomplish anything on our own or of our own accord. It is God who works in us through Holy Spirit and therefore all the Glory belongs to God. Isaiah reminds us that the infinite thoughts and the wondrous ways of God are so much greater than our finite minds and our futile ways. We have to know and acknowledge that we are the creation and Jehovah Elohim is our creator. Giving God the glory is so imperative. I am reminded of the story in Acts 12 where King Herod Agrippa was so enthralled with the praises of the people. He did not give honor and glory to God. King Herod Agrippa was immediately struck with sickness and consumed with worms. We can do nothing at all on our own. It is by the grace of God that we wake each morning. It is by God's mercy that we have our mental faculties. We don't even belong to ourselves because we were bought with a high price and we must use our bodies to glorify God (1 Corinthians 6:20). 1 Corinthians 10:31 calls for us to give God the glory in everything we do. Our lives are a reflection of the very name of God and he means to make His name great. That should be our daily prayer. Lord use me to make Your name great! Besides we are the royal priesthood, God's holy possession and we should display His goodness since He has called us out of darkness. (1 Peter 2:9). In Revelations 4, John sees a heavenly vision of four living creatures and the 24 Elders worshipping God on His throne. God is the center of attention. They keep their focus on God alone. The Elders dropped to their faces and cast their crowns before the throne of God. They made sure to give all of the Glory to God. They didn't even want the glory that God had given to them to take precedence over the glory due to His name. We must be careful to not take as our own the glory that is due to God. Men near and far are going to encounter the love of God by the way we stay in God's presence, guard our hearts from the schemes of the enemy, know who we are in Christ, take charge, have a surrendered spirit, use Godly restraint, and give all of the Glory to God.

WHO CAN RIVAL GOD?

"The LORD God tolerates no rivals; he punishes those who oppose him. In his anger he pays them back. The LORD does not easily become angry, but he is powerful and never lets the guilty go unpunished. Where the LORD walks, storms arise; the clouds are the dust raised by his feet!"

Nahum 1:2-3 GNB

God is eternal. He is all powerful, self-existing, and a mighty God, yet so full of love, grace and mercy. In Revelations 1:8 The Lord God says, "I am the Alpha and the Omega, the beginning and the end.... I am the One who is, Who always was, and who is still to come, the Almighty One". He is El Shaddai The Almighty God (Genesis 17:1). The enemy wants to imitate our God but can never measure up. There is no other God-there never has been and there will never be (Isaiah 43:10). Even Paul recognized the deceitfulness of the enemy in 2 Corinthians 11 "Even Satan disguises himself as an angel of light". The question is Who can rival God? The word rival is defined as a person or thing competing with another for the same objective or for superiority in the same field of activity (dictionary.com). Is there anyone or anything that can compete with our God? The answer is NO! So many things and people want to take first place in our lives but that place should always belong to God. He is Adoni our Lord; Elohim our Creator, and Jehovah God, who is in full control. God is all seeing and all knowing. He is self-existing and omnipresent. Job came to the realization that God is greater than we can ever understand (Job 36:26).

There is no one like the Lord, our God. Before the mountains were born, before you gave birth to the earth and the world, from beginning to end, you are God (Psalms 90:2). He is El Olam, the Everlasting God. We see in Nahum that God will not tolerate anyone or anything that attempts to oppose Him. The very first commandment given to the people from God was that they should have no other god before Him (Exodus 20:2). This still holds true for us today. There are so many obvious things that we can quickly and easily identify as idols but there are so many others that may seem harmless yet they can take precedence (ranked in front) over God.

Some of these things may be our jobs, relationships, children or success. It could also be one of our favorite pastimes like watching television shows, sporting events or playing games for an endless amount of time on our phones, computers or tablets. These things in themselves are not the problem. The problem is when they take a higher rank over us spending time with God. Have you ever found yourselves scrolling from one page to another on social media and yet we can't find the time to spend with God in prayer? In Ezekiel 28 we see God speaking through the prophet Ezekiel to the King of Tyre. This king, caught up in the spirit of pride, claimed himself as god. He boasted of his wisdom and his beauty. God clearly lets this pompous king know that He is the only true and living God by removing His hand of protection and allowing the foreign armies to bring terror to Tyre. We also see here in these verses that God is not only speaking to the human king but also to satan who is clearly at work in the King of Tyre. The devil himself has tried and failed to oppose The Most High God. Jesus tells us in Luke 10:18 how He saw Lucifer fall from Heaven like lightning. Now we see how the intent of the enemy is to see us have the same fate. The enemy wants to keep us so consumed with the cares of this world instead of keeping our eyes on our Creator.

Before we look into the character of our Father, I wanted to tell you some things about the great opposer, satan. Jesus reminds us in John 10 that the enemy comes but to kill, steal and destroy. The enemy is always looking for ways to destroy us. The enemy prowls around like a roaring lion seeking who he can devour. In Nehemiah chapters 4 and 6 we see how he plots against us and God's plans towards us. Nehemiah Chapter 4 shows us that while his enemies scoffed, Nehemiah prayed and continued to work (One hand with a sword, the other hand with tools). This is what we should be doing-talking to God about our situations (things that may try to hinder us or discourage us) but continue to do the work He sent us to do and allow God to fight the battle. Even if we have to work with a sword in our hands! Nehemiah was on the watch for the plots of his enemies and made changes as needed in order to continue working even in the midst (center) of opposition. Satan is not only a liar and a deceiver but he is the father of lies. When we fully know and trust in the character of God, we begin to see our lives and situations in a different light. Just like Nehemiah, he trusted what he heard the Word of the Lord say to him and he knew that despite the enemy's attempts to stop the work of the Lord, the work would be completed. The enemy always tries to imitate The Most High God but it is not his nature. He even disguises himself as an angel of light. The Word of God lets us know that we are not fighting against flesh and blood but against the evil rulers and authorities of the unseen world (Ephesians 6:12).

Every one of the Names of God we find in scripture not only describes who He is and the things He does for us but is an indelible part of His Being. We can see how the enemy works in our lives attempting to rival what God has said about us and about who He is in our lives. As we look at some of the names of God in scripture, we will begin to understand him more intimately and begin to trust Him like never before. The first name of God that we encounter in Genesis is Jehovah Elohim, God our creator. In Him is creation. In God there is creativity and with the breath that He breathed into us He also breathed creativity into us. When I researched the word creative or creativity it says that it is the use of the imagination; original ideas (dictionary.com). You are God's unique design. There is no one else like you and no one else with your purpose. John

1:4 says that the Word gave life to everything that was created. By His words the whole Earth came into order. He called forth the lights and they immediately obeyed. When God speaks something happens. Not only is He our creator but He is indeed our Lord, our Father. God is able to bring order to chaos. In the beginning we see what a mess the enemy had made of the earth. The Earth was void and full of darkness but by the words from the mouth of God He brought light into the darkness, formed and fill a formless and empty space, and called to order the water and land. God is still speaking in our lives today. He is willing to fill the empty spaces and bring light in the dark places of your life. He wants to bring order to your life today if you allow Him in. The only way we can truly see who we are is to look to the One who created us. No cheap imitation or chaotic situation can ever rival God.

Jehovah Jireh is one of the names of God mentioned in Genesis 22:14. Abraham was obedient to the end when God called for him to sacrifice his promised son. However, instead of Abraham's son being sacrificed God provided a ram to take Isaac's place. He is the Lord who sees, the One who provides. This is one of my favorite names (characteristics) of God. There are so many times in my life where He has richly provided for me. One particular time is when the house God blessed me with was in danger of foreclosure. My first response was complete devastation. I was thinking why would God bless me with this home and allow it to be taken away. Once I gathered my feelings, I realized that God is always faithful even when I was not the best steward over my blessings. I prayed to my Father and basically said, "Thy will be done". I was ready to do whatever He decided was best for me. I surrendered. In the end, I'm glad to say, God allowed me to remain in my home. He completely provided for me and He is ready to do the same for all of His children. God does not want us to worry about our needs because He will always take care of us. God proves Himself over and over again as the Great Provider. He sees all and knows all. If God provided oil and flour for the mother from Zarephath surely He will care and provide for us (1 Kings 17:8-15). We call Him omnipresent because He is everywhere and connected to everything. Am I a God who is only close at hand? Says the Lord. No, I am far away at the same time. Can anyone hide from me in a secret place?

Am I not everywhere in all the heavens and earth? (Jeremiah 23:23-24) What a blessing to serve the God who can see.

Not only does Jehovah Jireh see about our daily needs, but He also sees the things that we think are hidden. We are reminded in Isaiah 55 that God thinks differently from the way we think and the way He works is different from the way we work. God works from the inside out. After Saul was rejected by God, the prophet Samuel was sent to anoint the next king. Samuel thought he could easily identify the next king by the outward appearance. However, God reminded Samuel that He looks at the heart of man not his stature. God is intimate with us and He desires for us to have intimacy with Him. God not only sees what we need physically but more importantly He sees what we need spiritually. Matthew 6:25-31 lets us know that we can trust in Jehovah Jireh. If He provides for the animals and the flowers surely He will take care of our daily physical needs; all we need to do is seek Him. Don't look for the things, look for God. Along with God comes all of the things we need. It brings my heart so much joy to serve a God who can see me. There are times when I feel I can't form the words to fully express what I need, He already knows. Holy Spirit continuously prays on my behalf especially in the moments when I am too weak to pray for myself (Romans 8:26). Lack of any kind-whether it be physical, spiritual, or emotional-can never Rival God!

Another name for God is Jehovah Rophe – My Healer (Exodus 15:26); God indeed is my Healer. In Exodus 15 Miriam and the people of Israel sang a song of deliverance from Pharaoh and the degrading lifestyle of slavery in Egypt. It is here that God reveals Himself as the God who heals. God promises to keep them and that they will suffer none of the plagues He performed in Egypt if they will listen to and obey the voice of the Lord. This is the same promise God gives us today. Not only will God heal us from all manner of pestilence and disease, but He will also heal all spiritual, mental and heart afflictions as well. Jeremiah knows the healing power of God. He says in Jeremiah 17:14 that when God heals I will definitely be healed and when God saves He saves to the upmost. Whether God heals on this side of Heaven or the other side-God is a healer. Sickness of any kind whether it is physical, spiritual, or mental can never rival God! A third name for God is Jehovah Nissi – My Banner (Exodus 17:15); God declares to all the world that we belong to Him and that He fights on our behalf. He is Jehovah Nissi our Banner. This is the name Moses declared after the victory over the Amalekites. As long as Moses held up the staff given to him by God the Israelites were victorious but whenever he dropped his hands the Amalekites had the advantage. Aaron and Hur found a stone for Moses to rest on and they held up the hands of God's servant. This resulted in the Israelites gaining victory over the Amalekites. Moses gave God all of the Glory for this victory. During times of war, the troops would march towards the battle and on the front lines you would see the banner (flag) of whom they were representing. We as the soldiers of The Most High and we lift up God who reigns over us and God declares that He will fight for us. God has gone before us in battle and He has already won. It is because of God who is mighty in battle that we are victorious. After the victory over the Amalekites God instructed Moses to write it down as a permanent reminder. Moses was also instructed to read it out loud to Joshua. God reminds us to do the same thing. We have had many battles in our lives and experienced many victories. We should write them down as a permanent reminder and read them to the next generation as a testament of how God is there to fight for us. When the enemy comes in like a flood God holds up a standard against him. (Isaiah 59:19) It does not matter what troubles come your way. There have been so many times in my life that I've had to proclaim that it is God who protects me and I am His representative. He upholds His banner over me. None of our life battles can Rival God!

A fourth name for God is Jehovah Makadesh, who is God my Sanctifier, found in Leviticus 20:7-8. It is God that makes us Holy though we do have some work to do. The Word of the Lord declares that we must set ourselves apart. 2 Timothy 2 says that if we cleanse ourselves from what is dishonorable we will be a vessel for honorable use. We will be ready for every good work. So how exactly do we do this? We must turn away from sin and those who blatantly commit sin. 1 Corinthians 10:13 lets us know that the temptations in life are no different than what others experience. However, God is so faithful that he will not allow the temptation to be more than we can stand. When we are tempted, He will show us a way out so we can endure. Temptations will come but it is not the temptation that is sin. It is acting on the temptation that is sin. God does not and He will not negotiate with sin. It must be put to death. It says in Galatians 5:24 NLT that those who belong to Jesus have nailed the passions and desires of their sinful nature to His cross and crucified them there. We are a new creation and we have Holy Spirit who gives us the power to resist the devil and causes the devil to flee. Sin and the consequences of sin cannot rival God!

A fifth name for God is Jehovah Tsidkenu meaning God My Righteousness found in Jeremiah 23:6. God is righteous. What does it mean to be righteous? It means to be morally right, justifiable or virtuous. It is one of the chief attributes of God. We are told in 2 Corinthians 5:21 that we are made the righteousness of God through Jesus Christ. God in his mercy has made us right in His eyes. Jesus took our sin and nailed it to the cross and clothed us in righteousness. In Ephesians 6 God also gives us the breastplate of righteousness to proudly wear. It is because we are clothed in His righteousness that we enjoy the benefits of the Lord. In Isaiah 54:17 it says that because God has graciously wrapped us in His righteousness that no weapon formed against us shall prosper and every tongue that rises against us in judgment shall be condemned. When we abide in Christ we share in His inheritance; therefore, when He chose us and called us to Himself He gave us right standing declaring us free from the guilt of sin. He has also glorified us raising us to a heavenly dignity (Romans 8:30 AMP). The enemy loves to bring up the should haves, could haves, and would haves in our lives. He wants us to dwell on the mistakes of our past but in everything God will work it out for us. He will work it out for our good. When we stop looking at our shortcomings and our imperfections we can then look to the one who is able to do all things but fail. We can forgive ourselves and move forward. Even if we feel guilty, God is greater than our feelings, and He knows everything (1 John 3:20 NLT). Hold your heads up and walk tall because condemnation can never Rival God.

A sixth name for God is Jehovah Shalom, God is My Peace. In a world full of chaos, frustrations and strife, we definitely need Jehovah Shalom. We need to know the God, who is not only peace Himself, but is the giver of perfect peace. In Isaiah 26, God says that He will keep us in perfect peace if we trust Him and keep our thoughts fixed on Him. What are your eyes fixed on? If it is your situations or circumstances, then you need to adjust your gaze. Are you trusting in your abilities or great talents? Then you are trusting in vain. In order to experience His perfect peace, we must keep our eyes on our Heavenly Father, Jehovah Shalom. Not only is it necessary to keep looking to our Father but we must also unequivocally trust Him. We must have faith that He knows this is the right path for us. We must trust that He has our relationships and our children in His hands. As the phase goes we must "let go and let God". It's not that we're saying whatever I give up; what we are saying is that we are putting our situations, our children, our job, and our future into the hands of the One who can do something with it and make it good.

Jesus says in John 14 My peace I give to you so we should not allow our hearts to be troubled or afraid. One of my favorite Bible stories is when Jesus and the disciples were out on the water crossing to the other side of the lake when a fierce storm came along. The waves began to toss the boat to and fro, while Jesus was sleeping in the back of the boat. I can completely understand the response from His disciples. I'm sure they were thinking, How in the world can you be asleep during this crazy storm? They woke Jesus up with a shout, "Teacher don't you care that we're going to drown?" These were experienced fishermen, yet they were extremely concerned about this storm and the danger they were in. When the disciples asked Jesus this question it shows that they were aware He was able to handle the storm that was about to capsize their boat. The Bible says when Jesus woke up he rebuked the winds by saying, " Peace be still". Jesus also scolded His disciples for their trepidation and lack of faith. In life we are going to be faced with many storms some large and some small. It is imperative we trust God and trust that he is going to take care of us regardless of what we see. Worry, fear and doubt can never rival God.

A seventh name for God is Jehovah Rohi, which is interpreted as God my Shepherd. Understanding the characteristics of an earthly shepherd demonstrates why David called God his Shepherd and why we should also. The shepherd was to keep track of the flock. They were responsible to protect the flock from potential predators and disease. The shepherd was also charged with guiding the flock in the right direction and providing all that the sheep needed. The shepherd would routinely shear the sheep. The shearing process took off excess wool. Excessive wool impedes the sheep's ability to regulate their own body temperature and can cause them to get so hot that they could die. The filth attracted by the excess wool could cause irritation, infections, and endanger the health of the sheep. Large amounts of wool could also immobilize the sheep because of physical obstacles in their path. Furthermore, due to the overabundance of wool they were also more susceptible to attacks from predators.

Can you see this is what our great Shepherd does for us? David paints a beautiful picture of our Eternal God as our Shepherd in Psalms 23. He says that God gives us everything we need. He gives us rest in beautiful places and guides us beside peaceful streams. It is because of this rest that Jehovah renews our strength. Even in the dark places we travel during our lifetime our Rohi is right there close beside us giving us comfort. When we ignorantly stray off of the path He has set before us, He lovingly puts us back on track with His great staff. Just when we think God has done enough for us, He feeds us right in front of those who seek our demise and declares we are His own. He chases us down with His goodness and unfailing love. It says in Isaiah 40:11 that He will tend to His flock and gather His lambs in His arms. God will carry us in His bosom and those who are still nursing (on milk) He will gently lead. There is none who is greater than our Heavenly Father. Who can rival God? He is the great Shepherd. He does exceedingly and more abundantly than any physical shepherd can ever do. He provides like no other, protects like no one else can, and he cares for us greater than we can imagine. God knows exactly how and when to "prune" us. He is Master and King. Can you trust that God is a good shepherd? Will you trust where He is leading you? We need to know that our Father knows what is best for us. His eyes are always on us. The spirit of heaviness and abandonment cannot Rival God!

An eighth name for God is Jehovah Shammah, which translates to God, my abiding presence, which means He is there with me (Ezekiel 48:35). There is nothing more reassuring than to know that our Heavenly Father is always there with us. Even if I walk away from God, He will never leave me. When I get frustrated with this life, He is always there for me. He is our abiding presence, our Jehovah Shammah. This is inherent to who He is and He cannot deny himself. Jehovah Shammah is related to the name Emmanuel (God with us). Romans 8:38 heralds that nothing can ever separate us from the love of God. God himself declares that He will never leave us nor forsake us and He will personally go ahead of us (Deuteronomy 31:6). This is His covenant promise to His children. God is so faithful even when we are unfaithful. No matter what lies the enemy may tell, God will never leave us alone. We are not in this life journey without a companion.

I love the story in 2 Kings 6:17 when Elisha prays that his servant's eyes are opened so he could see that there were more on their side than the vast army that surrounded them. I can never escape from your Spirit! I can never get away from your presence! If I go up to heaven, you are there; if I go down to the grave, you are there. If I ride the wings of the morning, if I dwell by the farthest oceans, even there your hand will guide me, and your strength will support me. I could ask the darkness to hide me and the light around me to become night-but even in darkness I cannot be hidden from you. To you the night shines as bright as day. Darkness and light are the same to you (Psalms 139:7-12 NLT). The enemy wants us to think we are all alone and fighting by ourselves. My prayer for you today is that the Lord opens your eyes so that you may know that He is Jehovah Shammah. Loneliness cannot Rival God!

Growing from drinking the milk of the Word to eating meat as a mature Christian is a continuous journey. God wants to stretch out in us and as He increases we decrease. God is light and in Him there is no darkness at all (1 John 1:5 NLT) and he desires to fill us with His glory so that we can represent Him well. As we continue reading and learning of our Heavenly Father, let us remain faithful growing in spiritual maturity until we meet Him face to face.

"I am writing to you who are God's children because your sins have been forgiven through Jesus. I am writing to you who are mature in the faith because you know Christ, who existed from the beginning. I am writing to you who are young in the faith because you have won your battle with the evil one." 1 John 2:12-13 NLT

REFERENCES

Holy Bible: English Standard Version (ESV).(2001). Crossway. Good News Publishers

Holy Bible: King James Bible (KJV). (n.d). YouVersion Bible App. (Original work published 1769)

Holy Bible: New Living Translation (NLT).(2004). Wheaton, Illinois. Tyndale House Publishers

Peterson, Eugene H. (1993, 2002, 2018). Message Bible. (MSG)Tyndale House Publishers, Inc.

Strong, James. (1890, 1986). Strong's Concordance. Abingdon Press.